The Battles of the Lord
Spiritual Warfare in the Life of the Believer

Book One

By E. Truman Herring

The Battles of the Lord
Spiritual Warfare in the Life of the Believer
By E. Truman Herring
© Copyright 2018, E. Truman Herring

Cover Photo 22731997 © Vladimir Nikulin | Dreamstime.com

Dedication

I had the privilege to teach the content of this book to pastors' conferences in India, Colombia, and Brazil. Most of these pastors minister where Satan has built mighty spiritual fortresses against the Gospel of Christ. They are called and sent by God to bring the Light of Christ into some of the darkest places on earth. These are God's frontline soldiers. They, like Joshua, are called to be a good soldier and claim by spiritual conquest new territory for Christ.

Every place that the sole of your foot will tread upon I have given you, as I said to Moses....
No man shall be able to stand before you all the days of your life; as I was with Moses, so I will be with you. I will not leave you nor forsake you...
Be strong and of good courage; do not be afraid, nor be dismayed, for the LORD your God is with you wherever you go. (Joshua 1:3, 5, 9)

Three of my best friends were with me in India, and all three have encouraged my faith as they have since marched forward establishing new ministries: Pastor Marshall Wolcott in India, businessman Brad Williams in Colombia, and dentist Dr. Mike Barnard in Brazil.

The faith and dedication of these pastors and laymen inspire me.

Other Books by Truman Herring

Growing Through the Storms
Growing Through the Storms (Volume II)
God's Greater Purpose in Christ
Strong Fruitful Fulfilled – Hannah's Journey
A Ministry that Pleases God
Responsive Hearts – Fine Tuning Our Hearts to God's Heart
Sound the Alarm – Does God Judge Nations? Does God Judge America?
Sound the Alarm – A Call to Prayer
The Journey Series – Book 1 – Building a Strong Foundation
The Journey Series – Book 2 – Growing Deeper

For more information, please visit us at
trumanherringministries.com

Table of Contents

Introduction: Welcome to the Battle

Where Do Our Battles Come From?

Are you going through a battle right now? Yeah, me too. We all face them. They're all around us. They are hard. They keep coming. And we're all affected by them.

Battles can either *make us* or *break us*. Our success in the battle depends on several things: primarily, our understanding of God, our heavenly Father. Do we really trust Him? Will we obey Him no matter what? Secondly, our understanding of the purpose of the battle. Battles can either make us *better* or *bitter*. Let's start by understanding where battles come from.

☐ Some of our battles are brought on by **circumstances**.

Need some examples? Have you ever experienced any of the following? Layoffs at work that result in unemployment. Cancer and other health-related issues that change the course of our lives or the lives of our loved ones. Physical destruction wrought by hurricanes or other natural disasters that leave our world crumbled. Whatever the sources, our circumstances are turned upside down, and we have a battle on our hands.

☐ Some of our battles are brought on by **sin**.

We're all too familiar with these battles. Substance abuse that results in addictions. Marital infidelity that ruins a marriage. Child abuse that harms innocent victims.

It didn't take long in human history for anger resulting in violence to rear its ugly head … with devastating results. Four short chapters into the Bible, we read the record of the first brothers. There must have been animosity and sibling rivalry along the way. It finally culminated when *Cain rose up against his brother Abel and killed him* (Genesis 4:8).

Sin wreaks havoc. And we battle against it and its results every day of our lives.

☐ Some of our battles fall into an entirely different category. They are the result of **spiritual warfare**.

They come in the form of battles initiated by the Devil who seeks to steal and kill and destroy (John 10:10). The apostle Paul himself wrote, *For we do not wrestle against flesh and blood, but against principalities, against powers, against the rulers of the darkness of this age, against spiritual hosts of wickedness in the heavenly places* (Ephesians 6:12).

Jesus fought Satan all His life. Before His public ministry began, *Jesus was led up by the Spirit into the wilderness to be tempted by the devil* (Matthew 4:1). As followers of Jesus, we are not exempt from spiritual battle. That's why Paul tells us to *put on the full armor of God* and be ready every day to fight the battles that are before us.

If God would somehow pull back the veil that separates the *seen* from the *unseen,* we would be shocked to see how much of the battle falls into this category of spiritual warfare. Satan is alive and well on planet earth. He does prowl about like a roaring lion, seeking whom he may devour. He is the enemy of our souls. And he is after you. You must be on the alert (1 Peter 5:8).

---

*If God would somehow pull back the veil that separates the **seen** from the **unseen**, we would be shocked to see how much of the battle falls into this category of spiritual warfare.*

My First Realization of Spiritual Warfare

As a young married man in college, I had just experienced revival in my walk with God. One day I grieved over a particular sin that God had convicted me of. I asked God to forgive me. I was sincere and looked inside for a feeling of assurance that I was forgiven. But I did not feel anything. I prayed again, with more intensity, asking God for forgiveness. Still, I felt nothing. I then began to beg God repeatedly for forgiveness, thinking the more I asked, the quicker I would find forgiveness. But the feelings of forgiveness still did not come. Now I felt desperate and pleaded with God to forgive me with promises that I would do better. In the midst of this pleading, my emotions were released with tears. After the emotional release, I felt better and free of the guilt. I went to bed thinking that God had indeed forgiven me.

The next day, out of the blue, I remembered my sin and felt guilty all over again. My thought was, *Lord, I thought you forgave me last night.* I walked around the campus that day with a cloud over my head, feeling condemned for my sin.

That night I got on my knees again and pleaded with God for forgiveness. Again, I felt nothing. I tried to rationalize why I should feel forgiven, but still I felt guilty. It was not until I was able to have an emotional release of tears again that I felt forgiven. I went to bed thinking surely the Lord has forgiven me now. However, the next day the memory and guilt of my sin returned, and once again I questioned if God had really forgiven me. That up-and-down process continued every day and night that week.

On Sunday, I was alone in the worship center when the pastor came in early. I asked, *"How do you know when God has forgiven you for a specific sin?"* Instead of giving me an answer, he asked me a question: *"What does God's Word say?"* Without hesitation I began to quote 1 John 1:9, *"If we confess our sins, He is faithful and just to forgive us of our sins and to cleanse us from all unrighteousness."* In the middle of quoting that verse, I received understanding.

The way that I had been quoting 1 John 1:9 all week was by placing the emphasis on my confession, *If we **confess** our sin He is faithful and just to forgive.* However, that Sunday morning the emphasis shifted from **confess** to the truth of God's character, ***He is faithful and just to forgive.*** I had been confessing my sin and then looking within myself to see if I felt forgiven instead of looking to God and His promise and simply believing that I was forgiven by faith and not feelings.

I was forgiven the very first time I asked God—nearly a week earlier. Why then did I struggle with guilt needlessly? I was under spiritual attack. Satan was using my feelings against me. I then realized that week of condemnation was spiritual warfare.

The next day my sin came to my mind again, but this time I recognized it as "a fiery dart of condemnation from Satan." I refused to feel guilty for that which God had forgiven and forgotten. Simply believing God's promise caused the condemnation to cease. What a liberating truth!

Since learning this lesson about forgiveness, many church members have come to me who were repeating my mistake. One of the questions I have learned to ask regarding discerning the difference between the sweet conviction of the Holy Spirit to His child and the condemnation of the world, the flesh, and the devil, is "How many times have you confessed to God that particular sin?" Some have said they confessed the same sin not for a week, as in my case, but for months and even years. What liberty they found when they discovered the difference between the conviction of the Holy Spirit and the condemnation of the enemy!

My friend, we are all in this spiritual battle together, and we must put on the *"whole armor of God."* One of the purposes of this book is to identify the common tactics of our spiritual enemy and discover the victory God has already provided for us in Christ.

Take a moment and do some serious reflection. Grab a pen and write out a list of the battles you are facing *right now.* Ask the Father, "What are the battles that are going on in my life right now?" Some will come to your mind immediately. To remember others, you may have to reflect for some time to be able to put a name on them. Once you do that, ask yourself, "Which categories do each of these battles fall in? What is their source? Are they circumstantial? Are they caused by sin? Or are they best described as a temptation and trial caused by Satan?" (Note: some battles may fall into one or more categories.)

Battles I'm Going Through Right Now	
The Battle	The Source

When You Are in a Battle, Don't Forget …

Whatever type of battle you are facing, you can know three things:

1. The battle is real.

    Don't get caught off guard. Don't fall asleep. Don't think, *This is just life. It's no big deal.* The battle is real. Your soul is at stake. If you don't know you're in a battle, you're going to lose.

2. Your response to the battle is critical.

    Whenever you get serious about growing spiritually, Satan will take notice. He will deploy demons and other people to stop you. You must be prepared. God calls you to trust Him in the midst of the battle. He calls you to obey Him no matter what your feelings are. And He calls you to learn the lessons from each battle that He wants to teach you.

3. The battle belongs to the Lord.

    He is in control. He is sovereign. He is working His purposes for your good, your growth, and His glory. Trust Him.

How to Grow Through a Battle

God's Word gives us specific instructions to prepare us for the battle. If we were to view the characters of the Bible as our examples, we would find that their lives could be outlined in seasons of their lives as **slaves, sons, servants, and soldiers.**

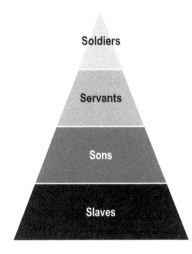

All were first and initially **slaves** to Satan and sin. Then God came and redeemed them and called them into a personal relationship as His **sons** and daughters. As His children, they all learned the lessons of humility and submission to God as His **servants**. They all were sent on mission as God's soldier to advance the Kingdom of God.

God illustrates men of faith in the Old Testament fighting God's battles against their strong enemies—not in their own strength but in the power of God. In the New Testament, we see that our warfare is spiritual. We lay down the swords of steel for the Sword of the Spirit, which is the Word of God.

These soldiers and the battles they face illustrate for us principles of spiritual warfare today. Abraham, Moses, Joshua, Caleb, Gideon, David, Asa, Jehoshaphat, Hezekiah, and many others fought the battles of the Lord not in their own strength but by faith through both the instructions and enabling of God.

If God's commission to the church were given in a closed system with no opposition, then spiritual warfare would not be so critical. But the world, Satan, and our own flesh oppose every advancement of the Kingdom of God in this world of darkness. We're in a very real battle.

But the world, Satan, and our own flesh oppose every advancement of the Kingdom of God in this world of darkness. We're in a very real battle.

For over twenty years, I've been intrigued with the battles in the Old Testament. Yes, they were physical battles. But they were so much more. As we will see, they were primarily spiritual battles. And they have great lessons for us today.

What you have in your hands is the first book in a series of books that will examine the battles recorded in Scripture. Though many Bible characters illustrate the role of a good soldier of Jesus Christ, this book will center on Joshua and how God used Moses to prepare him for leadership battles later in his life.

Joshua, Our Role Model

Joshua is perhaps the best illustration of how God prepares His sons to be servants and then to be soldiers on mission with God.

Chronologically, we see Joshua as a slave to Pharaoh, then as he spends forty years as a servant to God and Moses. Finally, he is sent by God as His soldier to fight the battles of the Lord in the conquest of the land of Canaan.

God very clearly instructed Moses to mentor Joshua and prepare him for his mission as a good soldier of God.

> *Joshua the son of Nun, who stands before you, he shall go in there.* **Encourage him**, *for he shall cause Israel to inherit it.* (Deuteronomy 1:38)

> *But* **command Joshua**, *and* **encourage him** *and* **strengthen him**; *for he shall go over before this people, and he shall cause them to inherit the land which you will see.* (Deuteronomy 3:28)

We're going to look at a section of Israel's early history and see how God took the nation from slavery in Egypt to freedom in the Promised Land. We'll see how Moses mentored Joshua to be the next-generation leader for Israel. We will begin in the book of Exodus and go all the way up to when Israel was prepared to conquer the Promised Land. A future book will pick up in Joshua chapter one and follow Joshua as he commands the troops to conquer the Land.

Joshua Trained for Warfare

Moses knew how to develop leaders. He knew that part of his calling was to train and develop a godly leader who would chart the course for the nation after he died. We are going to look at the stages and seasons of Joshua's training and preparation for warfare. And then we will focus on his leadership through the battles that occurred after Moses died.

How did Joshua fight battles? What did he learn? Joshua was trained in warfare by nine battles under Moses' leadership:

	The Battle	The Lesson
1	The Battle at the Red Sea against Pharaoh	The Soldier's Foundational Battle and Salvation by Grace
2	The Battle with Amalek	The Battle of Intercession: How the Lord Fights the Battle with Us
3	The Battle Within	Putting to Death Our Old, Sinful Desires
4	The Battle at Kadesh Barnea	The Battle of Retreat and the Danger of Fear Instead of Faith
5	The Battle at Arad	How Unexpected Attacks Can Bring Unexpected Blessings
6	The Battle with Sihon	How God Expands our Territory
7	The Battle with Og	A Pattern of Faith and Victory for the Future Battles
8	The Battle with Balak and Balaam	The Unseen Battle Behind the Scenes
9	The Battle with the Midianites	The Soldier's Bounty

Are You Ready?

Are you ready to learn how to fight? Grab your sword (that's the Word of God), put on your armor (Ephesians 6:10–18), and let's learn what it means to *fight the good fight*. And remember *… the battle belongs to the Lord.*

First Things First

You can't put the cart before the horse. This old-time saying reminds us of a very important principle: order is important. Horses aren't very good at pushing carts. It works much better if you have them *pull* the cart.

In the same way, order is important in God's work. Here's a critical principle to remember: *God must work **in us** before He can work **through us**.*

Here's a critical principle to remember:
*God must work **in us** before He can work **through us**.*

As we look at how God progressively prepared Joshua to be God's soldier-leader, it is important to get a sampling of Joshua's first two battles as an overview of how God recorded these battles for our learning today as soldiers of Christ called to advance God's kingdom.

Lessons from Joshua's First Battle at the Rea Sea

You'll see this diagram replicated throughout the book as we go through each of the battles Joshua faced. It gives us a visual reminder of what has happened in Joshua's progression of faith.

The Red Sea: Salvation by Grace

We will first look at the principles of spiritual warfare through the experience of what Joshua learned as God prepared him and led him in the conquest of the inheritance that God promised Abraham and his seed.

Then the LORD said to Moses, "Write this for a memorial in the book and recount it in the hearing of Joshua, that I will utterly blot out the remembrance of Amalek from under heaven." (Exodus 17:14)

It is clear that God was preparing Joshua to be His soldier. And did you notice what God specifically told Moses to do? *"Recount it in the hearing of Joshua."* Moses was to write this battle down and remind Joshua of it over and over.

Israel wrote down all their battles in what is called *The Book of War* (Numbers 21:14–15).[1] Israel's leaders were to study *The Book of War*. It is clear that David studied previous battles of Scripture (2 Samuel 11:20–21). Throughout history, great generals of war have studied the battles of history past to learn strategy for war tomorrow. And like Joshua, we must also learn the principles of spiritual warfare by studying the battles that God recorded for us in Scripture.

By the way, it is important to note that Joshua also presents to us a "type" of Christ in His victory over Satan. The book of Joshua with its theme of conquest and dividing of the inheritance after victory finds a parallel in the book of Ephesians with its declaration of our victory in Christ and His blessing our inheritance in Him.

> *The book of Joshua with its theme of conquest and dividing of the inheritance after victory finds a parallel in the book of Ephesians with its declaration of our victory in Christ and His blessing our inheritance in Him.*

The first battle that Joshua experienced in his training with Moses was the most important battle of all. It was the foundational battle for all future battles he would face. The lessons we apply from this battle are also foundational to all our spiritual warfare. No soldier of Christ can advance the Kingdom of God without understanding its principles.

The Context of the First Battle

When God first began to fulfill His promise to Abraham, He sent Moses to deliver the Hebrews from the bondage of Pharaoh. Pharaoh challenged God, *"Who is the Lord that I should obey him?"* and with a hardened heart, he refused to release his slaves. That wasn't a smart move.

Going against the King of heaven and earth resulted in a series of plagues and devastating events that would demonstrate the power of Almighty God. And everyone took notice: the Egyptians, the Israelites, and the nations of Canaan whom Joshua would later conquer, all realized that God was all-powerful and going up against Him was useless. The ten plagues of God devastated Egypt. And finally, Pharaoh released the Hebrew slaves.

---

[1] *The Book of the Wars of the Lord* is one of several non-canonical books referenced in the Bible which have now been completely lost. They were not part of God's inspired and true Word, but they were books of history that certainly captured the works of the Lord in that day.

After the Israelites fled, Pharaoh hardened his heart again. He regretted releasing the Hebrews and sent his army to make them turn back or be destroyed.

Enter the obstacle.

Every battle starts with something. This one started with an obstacle—a wet one. As Israel marched forward, they saw the water. Perhaps they heard the waves. The Red Sea.

Technically, the Red Sea is a seawater inlet of the Indian Ocean, lying between Africa and Asia. But emotionally, it was a crusher. It took the Israelites' dreams of freedom and hope and dashed them against the shoreline.

> *The Israelites' dreams of freedom and hope*
> *were dashed against the shoreline of the Red Sea.*

Exodus 14:4 gives us a behind-the-scenes insight that we wouldn't have expected. God said, *"Thus I will harden Pharaoh's heart, and he will chase after (the Israelites)."* Don't miss that: **God Himself** engineered the circumstances. **He** hardened Pharaoh's heart. **He** initiated the chase.

Was this some sort of cosmic joke? Did God have a bad day and say, *"Hey Israel. Forget all My promises. I've changed My mind. You really angered Me, and I'm going to let you die in the wilderness."*

NO! God knew what He was doing ... and He knows what He is doing in your life.

> *God knew what He was doing ... and He knows what He is doing in your life.*

The question is ... how will you respond when you can't explain the inexplainable? What do you do when you can't fathom the unfathomable?

Joshua walked in faith, but most of the Israelites were fickle and walked in fear. When they saw blessings, they praised God. But when they were tested, they murmured against God. This was true at the Red Sea, as the praise of God for their deliverance quickly turned into fearful complaints.

> *So they were very afraid, and the children of Israel cried out to the LORD. Then they said to Moses, "Because there were no graves in Egypt, have you taken us away to die in the wilderness? Why have you so dealt with us, to bring us up out of Egypt? Is this not the word that we told you in Egypt, saying, 'Let us alone that we may serve the Egyptians'? For it would have been better for us to serve the Egyptians than that we should die in the wilderness."* (Exodus 14:10–12)

Murmuring and complaining became Israel's consistent refrain, one that Moses and Joshua would have to deal with all their lives. Oh, and just in case you didn't make the application, we face the same challenges today: *to fully trust God, to remain positive, and to not despair.* Here are two critical points for us to remember as followers and leaders:

1. It is so easy for us, as Jesus-followers today, to fall into the same trap of murmuring and complaining. We see God work. He miraculously delivers and answers our prayers. And two days later, we forget all about those blessings and go back to being negative and again start fretting about the future. The hymn writer said it well, "Prone to wander, Lord I feel it. Prone to leave the God I love." Quit complaining! Stop the murmuring! God's got it. He's in control.

> *The hymn writer said it well, "Prone to wander, Lord I feel it. Prone to leave the God I love." Quit complaining! Stop the murmuring! God's got it. He's in control.*

2. As leaders of people that are prone to wander, we have to keep calling them back to the faithfulness and greatness of God.

Joshua learned that he not only had to battle the enemies outside the camp like Pharaoh, but also he would have to battle those within the camp, God's own people, who say: *"Let us alone that we may serve the Egyptians."* (Young leaders, you must quickly learn that there are not only battles *outside* the church but *inside* the church as well. And the battles *inside* are much more deadly.)

The battle instructions that God gave Moses place the focus entirely on God for victory. It wasn't on the soldiers. It wasn't the strategy that would save them. *It was the Lord.* When we say that the battle belongs to the Lord, there is no better illustration of this principle than here in Exodus 14:13–14.

> *And Moses said to the people, "Do not be afraid. Stand still, and see the salvation of the LORD, which He will accomplish for you today. For the Egyptians whom you see today, you shall see again no more forever. The LORD will fight for you, and you shall hold your peace."*

Israel watched as God divided the Red Sea, and they went over on dry ground. As they were pursued by Pharaoh and his army, God let the wall of water collapse on the Egyptians. Israel stood still and saw the salvation of the Lord. He fought for them, and they watched the Lord defeat their enemy. They did *nothing.* God did *everything.* Imagine the kind of faith that was built in Joshua who was being prepared to do the same thing at the crossing of the Jordan and at Jericho. The more Joshua rehearsed that day in his mind, the stronger his faith became.

> *Imagine the kind of faith that was built in Joshua who was being prepared to do the same thing at the crossing of the Jordon and at Jericho. The more Joshua rehearsed that day in his mind, the stronger his faith became.*

God has given us a similar experience through our salvation. The longer we stand still and remember the great work of Christ on the Cross and at the empty tomb, the stronger our faith grows to experience victory over Satan.

The First Battle Was Foundational for All Future Battles

This first battle gave Joshua foundational principles of warfare for trusting God in the conquest of the Promised Land. We should see some spiritual principles for us as well.

1. *"Fear not"* is the attitude of the soldier in spiritual battle.
2. *"Stand still"* is the position of the soldier in spiritual battle.
3. *"See the salvation of the Lord"* is the object of the soldier's faith.
4. *"The Lord shall fight for you"* is the promise of the soldier in spiritual battle.
5. *"You shall hold your peace"* is the soldier ceasing from his own strength to enter into the victory of "God's rest."

This battle is foundational for all future battles that Joshua would face. It is much like our salvation. We do not fight *for* victory first, but *from* the victory already won for us through Christ. Let's look at each of these principles individually.

1. *"Fear not"* is the attitude of the soldier in spiritual battle.

Fear was the natural state when Israel faced its many battles. Fear is also a real emotion that we all face. Fear was present at the Red Sea, and it was present when the ten spies gave an evil report because they saw the giants of Canaan. In the battles Israel faced, God raised up a leader who faced his fears with faith and calmed the fears of the army. Joshua was such a man, and he would repeat these words to Israel (Numbers 14:9).

All of us will face circumstances that will bring out fear. We also have our emotions that go up and down with circumstances. This does not mean we are disqualified for battle. But it does mean that we can be disqualified if we do not overcome fear with faith (Deuteronomy 20:8).

It is up to us to make a choice to resist this fear and stand on God's Word and exercise faith. "Fear not" is not a *suggestion* but a *command* from God. When God commands, He gives enabling grace to obey. One key to overcome our natural fear is to fear God more than the enemy we face. We do that by believing and putting our trust in God (Exodus 14:31).

18

*Thus Israel saw the great work, which the LORD had done in Egypt; **so the people feared the LORD, and believed the LORD** and His servant Moses* (Exodus 14:31, emphasis mine).

God is aware of the natural fear we face when our circumstances look overwhelming. Consider the sampling of just a few of the many passages where God encourages us to make a choice between fear and faith.

- Moses was a man of faith, but God continually encouraged him not to fear.

  Then the LORD said to Moses, "Do not fear him, for I have delivered him into your hand, with all his people and his land; and you shall do to him as you did to Sihon king of the Amorites, who dwelt at Heshbon (Numbers 21:34).

- Moses encouraged Joshua not to fear.

  *And I commanded Joshua at that time, saying, "Your eyes have seen all that the LORD your God has done to these two kings; so will the LORD do to all the kingdoms through which you pass. **You must not fear them**, for the LORD **your God Himself fights for you**"* (Deuteronomy 3:21–22, emphasis mine).

  *"Be strong and of good courage, **do not fear** nor be afraid of them; for the LORD your God, He is the One who goes with you. He will not leave you nor forsake you"* (Deuteronomy 31:6, emphasis mine).

- God encouraged Joshua not to fear.

  *So Joshua ascended from Gilgal, he and all the people of war with him, and all the mighty men of valor. And the LORD said to Joshua, "**Do not fear them**, for I have delivered them into your hand; not a man of them shall stand before you"* (Joshua 10:7–8, emphasis mine).

- Moses encouraged Israel to drive out the nations of Canaan, but they feared and turned back.

  *And I said to you, "You have come to the mountains of the Amorites, which the LORD our God is giving us. Look, the LORD your God has set the land before you; go up and possess it, as the LORD God of your fathers has spoken to you; **do not fear or be discouraged**."* (Deuteronomy 1:20–21, emphasis mine).

- God reminded them not to let the large numbers of the enemy cause them to fear.

  *When you go out to battle against your enemies, and see horses and chariots and people more numerous than you, **do not be afraid of them**; for the LORD your God is with you, who brought you up from the land of Egypt* (Deuteronomy 20:1, emphasis mine)

☐ God reminded them not to faint, be afraid, tremble, or be terrified in the day of battle because the Lord was with them to fight for them.

*And he shall say to them, "Hear, O Israel: Today you are on the verge of battle with your enemies. Do not let your heart faint, **do not be afraid**, and do not tremble or be terrified because of them; for the LORD your God is He who goes with you, to fight for you against your enemies, to save you"* (Deuteronomy 20:2–4, emphasis mine).

☐ If a soldier could not overcome his fear with faith, he was disqualified to be in God's army and was sent home.

*The officers shall speak further to the people, and say, "What man is there who is **fearful** and fainthearted? Let him go and return to his house, lest the heart of his brethren faint like his heart"* (Deuteronomy 20:8, emphasis mine).

This fear became contagious on the battlefield.

☐ The soldier learns to fear God more than his enemy. As he learns about God in the Word, he grows in faith by his obedience to it.

*If you do not carefully observe all the words of this law that are written in this book, **that you may fear this glorious and awesome name,** THE LORD YOUR GOD* (Deuteronomy 28:58, emphasis mine).

Gather the people together, men and women and little ones, and the stranger who is within your gates, that they may hear and that they may learn to fear the LORD your God and carefully observe all the words of this law (Deuteronomy 31:12).

The first time I shared the Gospel one-on-one, I was nervous and afraid. When God called me to preach, I used the excuse that I could not speak well. I was afraid. I have now preached for forty-seven years, and I still face fear before I stand in the pulpit. The same could be said for personal evangelism. After all these years, I still have to battle fear before I go. Perhaps this natural fear should remind us all that we must, as an act of our will, exercise faith in the Lord and be dependent upon Him and not our own strength.

I am sure that soldiers who went into battle were afraid, but they chose duty over their fears. The soldier must learn the difference between fear as a part of our flesh, fear as an emotion, and the faith that obeys God in spite of our emotions. *"Fear not"* is a command. And what God commands He enables us to do. We must use our will to say *no* to our emotional fears. Do not let fear become an excuse to keep you out of service to the Lord.

Do not let fear become an excuse to keep you out of service to the Lord.

---

2. *"Standing still"* is the position of the soldier in spiritual battle.

Our flesh drives us to either *flee in fear* or to *rush ahead in pride*. The soldier must overcome both of these reactions. God taught Joshua that victory is all about the grace and power of God. When God lays the foundation of victory by salvation, we have no part in it but to stand still and see the salvation of God. We cannot lift our swords in this battle, for we are told to do *nothing*. And the glory from this victory cannot be claimed by us, for it is God's doing. We are saved by grace alone and by God alone.

> *Our flesh drives us to either flee in fear or to rush ahead in pride.*

Joshua stood still and saw the salvation of the Lord. And it was the foundation for all his future victories and the conquest of the Promised Land.

As Joshua stood there and watched God defeat his enemies, it created faith to defeat his fear, humility to battle his pride, and resulted in praise to God to quench the future praise from men for his future victories.

Most who were there with Joshua would not be permanently impacted as he was. They stood still and observed … but they were not changed as he was. That generation would be tested ten times from that day until their final act of fear and unbelief at Kadesh Barnea as they believed the evil report of the ten spies and rejected the report of faith from Joshua and Caleb. Because of their unbelief, God let them live in failure for forty years in the wilderness until that generation had all died.

There is a time to fight … but it follows learning the principle of first standing still. Joshua will indeed fight in the next battle, but it will be with dependence upon God.

The Pattern of Salvation

This first foundational battle in grace carries the pattern of our salvation in grace as well.

- We are saved by grace and not by our works (Ephesians 2:8–9).
- We cease from our works to enter His finished work and enjoy the rest of salvation (Hebrews 4:10).
- Jesus became the Last Adam to represent us, and it was by His obedience alone that we were made righteous (Romans 5:18–19).

God has given us a firm foundation in Christ, and it is on this foundation that we build and battle in the future.

> *God has given us a firm foundation in Christ,*
> *and it is on this foundation that we build and battle in the future.*

☐ We now stand because we were justified by faith.

   Therefore, having been justified by faith, we have peace with God through our Lord Jesus Christ, through whom also we have access by faith into this grace in which we stand, and rejoice in hope of the glory of God (Romans 5:1–2).

☐ Christ freed us from the slavery to Satan and sin. We stand in that victory that He obtained for us.

   Stand fast therefore in the liberty by which Christ has made us free, and do not be entangled again with a yoke of bondage (Galatians 5:1)

Stand Still and Wait on God

This concept of first *standing still* means that we wait on God in prayer and read God's Word before we rush ahead. God must speak first … and then we move.

Joshua learned that God had instructed Israel that its commander should stand before the high priest and ask direction from God. Later, we will see that when Joshua waited on God, God directed him in battle. But when he forgot, when he did not ask counsel of the Lord, he was defeated by his enemy (Joshua 9:14).

> *When Joshua waited on God, then God directed him in battle, but when he forgot, when he did not ask counsel of the Lord, then he was defeated by his enemy.*

To wait on God is to be dependent upon God for direction and for power.

   But they that wait upon the LORD shall renew their strength; they shall mount up with wings as eagles; they shall run, and not be weary; and they shall walk, and not faint (Isaiah 40:31).

There are still three more principles to learn from this incident, and we'll continue this study in the next chapter.

 **Application**

Spiritual warfare and the assurance of salvation:

Every believer will face the common spiritual battle of being attacked over the assurance of salvation. After a great salvation testimony is given at church, some have come to me with doubt, saying, "I do not remember all the specific details of my salvation testimony like him." After a great sin, some have asked, "How could I be saved and have done such a thing?" The attacks of the assurance of salvation are many.

To win this battle we must always "stand still at the Cross." We must not try to prove that we are saved by remembering every detail of our salvation testimony. The battle would be endless: "How do you know you were sincere enough? How do you know that you really repented? How do you know your feelings were not just emotions?

Instead, we find assurance on a sure foundation in Christ's finished work in our behalf. Our focus must not first be on any part of what we did but simply believing and thanking God for what Christ did in our place.

Lord Jesus, thank You that You died for sinners. I am a sinner. Thank You that Your death saved me.

Write below a statement in this section that spoke to you.

A Quick Review

The Red Sea:
Salvation by
Grace

We began our study of the Battle at the Red Sea in the previous chapter, where we talked about the first two critical principles:

1. **"Fear not" is the attitude of the soldier in spiritual battle.**

   The soldier must learn the difference between fear as a part of our flesh, fear as an emotion, and the faith that obeys God in spite of our emotions. *"Fear not"* is a command. And what God commands He enables us to do. We must use our will to say *no* to our emotional fears. Do not let fear become an excuse to keep you out of service to the Lord.

2. **"Standing still" is the position of the soldier in spiritual battle.**

   Joshua learned that God had given instruction to Israel before going to war that its commander should stand before the high priest and ask direction from God. We will later see that when Joshua waited on God, then God directed him in battle, but when he forgot, when he did not ask counsel of the Lord, then his enemy defeated him (Joshua 9:14).

   To wait on God is to be dependent upon God for direction and for power.

   > *But those who wait upon the LORD shall renew their strength; they shall mount up with wings as eagles; they shall run, and not be weary; and they shall walk, and not faint* (Isaiah 40:31).

   Once we know that our victory is in the Lord alone, then we are ready to enter into spiritual warfare. Not before.

Three More Lessons from Joshua's First Battle at the Rea Sea

3. *"See the salvation of the Lord"* is the object of the soldier's faith.

Standing still is linked with *seeing*. Standing still is not empty inactivity. It is not making soldiers passive for the battle. It is part of the grace and faith process to prepare the soldier for victory.

> *Standing still is not empty inactivity. It is not making soldiers passive for the battle. It is part of the grace and faith process to prepare the soldier for victory.*

Our standing still in a posture of faith must be connected to *"seeing the salvation of the Lord."* Unless we have the proper object of faith (God Himself), then both our standing still and seeing are in vain.

Seeing a miracle does not guarantee that the end result will be lasting faith. The multitudes saw the miracles of Jesus and ate the multiplied loaves and fishes but rejected His message and left Him. Moses delivered God's promise of deliverance and the signs God gave him, and Exodus 4:31 reports that the Hebrew slaves believed and worshiped. However, when Pharaoh reacted to God's message by increasing their labor and suffering, they complained to Moses. Their faith was fickle.

That generation had the same fickle faith at the Rea Sea. They had seen God's victory over Pharaoh. Like Joshua, they stood still and saw the salvation of the Lord. However, most of them did not see what Moses, Joshua, Caleb, and other faithful Hebrews saw. Joshua saw with the eyes of faith and perceived. He saw deeper, beyond the surface, and understood what God was doing.

> *He saw deeper, beyond the surface, and understood what God was doing.*

Some "see to believe." Some see and cannot believe their own eyes. Some see and do not perceive. God summed up the majority history of Israel's seeing this way:

> *The word of the LORD also came unto me, saying, "Son of man, thou dwellest in the midst of a rebellious house, which have eyes to see, and see not; they have ears to hear, and hear not: for they are a rebellious house."* (Ezekiel 12:1–2)

> *And He said, "Go, and tell this people: 'Keep on hearing, but do not understand; keep on seeing, but do not perceive.'"* (Isaiah 6:9)

Moses reproved those who stood that day at the Red Sea. They saw what Joshua and Caleb saw but did not believe like they believed.

Now Moses called all Israel and said to them: "You have seen all that the LORD did before your eyes in the land of Egypt, to Pharaoh and to all his servants and to all his land—the great trials which your eyes have seen, the signs, and those great wonders. Yet the LORD has not given you a heart to perceive and eyes to see and ears to hear, to this very day. (Deuteronomy 29:2–4)

Some "believe to see" by making the Lord the object of their faith.

Joshua made the Lord Himself the object of his faith, while most of Israel only focused on their physical deliverance from slavery. They demonstrated their unbelief over and over in the wilderness journey. And when they came to the border of the Promised Land, they saw giants who were so big that they could not see the salvation of the Lord.

Joshua had double vision. He could see what the evil spies saw, but he also could see what they could not see. He had discovered the deep lesson of believing God's promises and seeing beyond the circumstances to the Lord Himself.

Once Joshua had the proper object of faith, he had 20/20 spiritual vision. While the evil spies saw themselves as grasshoppers compared to the giants, Joshua and Caleb saw the same God they saw at the Rea Sea. They had a foundation for every battle and all the changing circumstances they would ever face. They settled the issue in one moment at the Red Sea: their God would be sufficient for all they would face in the future.

If God could open the Red Sea and defeat Pharaoh and his army, then for Joshua it was settled forever and for every situation that he would face. God would be to Joshua at the Jordan and at the battle of Jericho what he was at the Red Sea—the Lord of salvation.

Seeing with the eye of faith is explained in this quote from A. W. Pink:

> *Heb. 11:29 tells us that it was "by faith they passed through the Red Sea," and faith is the opposite of sight. The mistake arises from jumping to the conclusion that "see the salvation of the Lord" refers to physical sight. It was spiritual sight that Moses referred to, the exercising of the eyes of the heart. Faith is a looking not at the things which are seen, but a looking "at the things which are not seen" (2 Cor. 4:18).... And of Moses we read, "he endured as seeing Him who is invisible" (Heb. 11:27) that is, seeing Him with the eyes of faith. To "see the salvation of the Lord" we must first "stand still"—all fleshly activity must cease.*[2]

To "see the salvation of the Lord" we must first "stand still"—
all fleshly activity must cease.
---

[2] Pink, A.W. (1964). *Gleanings in Joshua* (pp. 177–202). Chicago: Moody Press.

With every attack, temptation, or problem, we should first stand still for a moment and stand on the foundation Jesus has already laid for us by His victory. We are strengthened in our faith as we remember the day of our salvation. We see and perceive again and again what Jesus accomplished for us.

Our victory took place at the Cross. We should stand there often and remember:

☐ Jesus' obedience and righteous life made Him God's perfect sacrifice. He was worthy.

☐ His perfect substitutionary death took our place in judgment. The Gospel can be summed up in four simple words: *Jesus in my place*.

☐ His conquest over death through the resurrection proved His victory.

☐ His faithful position of Advocate and High Priest for us in heaven gives me confidence in prayer.

The true soldier of Jesus Christ must never forget what he saw with the eye of faith and understanding when the Lord saved him.

4. *"The Lord shall fight for you"* is the promise of the soldier in spiritual battle.

Why did the Lord fight for Israel? Why will He fight for you?

The answer is very simple: because of His grace and His great love for you. Remind yourself of that truth often … but especially when you are in the midst of the battle. Never forget that.

> *Why should the Lord fight for Israel? Why should He fight for you? The answer is very simple: because of His grace and His great love for you.*

The Lord shall fight for you because He chose Abraham and made a promise to him, and this day of battle is part of that great promise of deliverance from Egypt.

In preparation for his commission as a good soldier, Joshua is told to *"Stand still and hold his peace."* It would be like a commanding officer telling a soldier, *"Soldier, stand down and do nothing."* In our context, Joshua was told that the Lord alone would fight for him. He was not supposed to take any action in this battle … only to believe.

Why did the Lord choose to fight this battle alone? Because there was no one else capable of accomplishing what God desired. Who else could open the Rea Sea so Israel might be set free? Who else could send ten supernatural plagues on Egypt to get Pharaoh's attention? Joshua learned to trust God completely, so much so that in a future battle he would command the sun to stand still in the heavens.

This was a faith-building day for Joshua. It was also a glory-getting day for the Lord. Everyone everywhere would hear of His great power to deliver His nation.

At the Red Sea, Joshua forever settled in his mind that God was the God of the impossible. What God promised to perform, He accomplished. That which He commanded, He enabled Joshua to obey. Where He sent His soldier, He provided.

There are some things that only God alone can do. He doesn't need our help—and besides, we are powerless to help Him anyway.

- Only God could create the world out of nothing. We cannot.

  O LORD of hosts, God of Israel, the One who dwells between the cherubim, You are God, You alone, of all the kingdoms of the earth. You have made heaven and earth. (Isaiah 37:16)

- Only God is immortal and eternal. We are finite and mortal.

  He who is the blessed and only Potentate, the King of kings and Lord of lords, who alone has immortality, dwelling in unapproachable light, whom no man has seen or can see, to whom be honor and everlasting power. Amen. (1 Timothy 6:15–16)

- Only God deserves honor and glory for His great work. We do not.

  The lofty looks of man shall be humbled, the haughtiness of men shall be bowed down, and the LORD alone shall be exalted in that day. (Isaiah 2:11)

  Now to the King eternal, immortal, invisible, to God who alone is wise, be honor and glory forever and ever. Amen. (1 Timothy 1:17)

- Only the Lord could die to save us from our sins. We cannot save ourselves.

  [Jesus], who being the brightness of His glory and the express image of His person, and upholding all things by the word of His power, when He had by Himself purged our sins, sat down at the right hand of the Majesty on high. (Hebrews 1:3)

Joshua learned that with God nothing is impossible.

Joshua stood still and saw the Lord fight for him and do the impossible. He believed that no matter what great enemies and obstacles he faced in the future, the Lord could do the impossible and fight for him.

God asked Abraham,
"Is there anything too hard for the Lord?" (Genesis 18:14)

God asked Jeremiah the same question. *"Behold, I am the LORD, the God of all flesh. Is there anything too hard for Me? (Jeremiah 32:26–27).*

When Mary wondered how she could give birth to the Messiah while a virgin, God answered, *"With God nothing shall be impossible"* (Luke 1:37).

From the Red Sea Battle to the Battle at the Cross

Just as Joshua stood still at the Red Sea and saw the salvation of the Lord, we must stand still and see the salvation of the Lord at the Cross.

Jesus alone fought for us to obtain our salvation. He alone is unique and qualified to be the one to fight for us and obtain for us eternal salvation. He alone is fully God. Yet He was also fully man to represent us. The Messiah had to be born of a virgin with no earthly father so as not to inherit the sin nature of our father, Adam.

In this unique role, Jesus did for us what we could not do. He faced Satan and temptation and never sinned. As God's sinless man, He alone qualified to be the Lamb of God to take away the sin of the world.

> *For as by one man's disobedience many were made sinners, so also by one Man's obedience many will be made righteous.* (Romans 5:19)

As God's sinless man, Jesus alone qualified
to be the Lamb of God to take away the sin of the world.

The soldier of God must stand still and see the great salvation that the Lord Jesus alone obtained.

- We could not defeat Satan. But Jesus came to destroy the works of the Devil.

- We could not free ourselves, for we were born slaves to sin. But Jesus came to redeem us with His blood.

☐ We could not live sinless lives and stand before a Holy God. *"But Jesus, who knew no sin, became sin for us, that we might be made the righteousness of God in Him"* (2 Corinthians 5:21).

☐ We could not pay the penalty for our sin, which is death. *But while we were sinners Christ died for us* (Romans 5:8).

☐ We could not conquer death, but on the third day Jesus arose to become our Resurrection and Life.

We must stand still and see that salvation is impossible to us, but possible only in the Lord Jesus.

The rich young ruler came to Jesus, questioning how to obtain eternal life. *"What good thing shall I do that I might have eternal life?"* (Matthew 19:16). Jesus answered that salvation was too hard for man. In fact, it was impossible.

> *And those who heard it said, "Who then can be saved?" But He said, "The things which are impossible with men are possible with God"* (Luke 18:26–27).

As soldiers, we stand at the Cross and, in deep love and humility, acknowledge these great truths —that the Lord alone saved us and that we could do nothing but receive this gift of grace from Jesus Christ by faith.

The Lord alone saved us.
We could do nothing but receive this gift of grace from Jesus Christ by faith.

Like Joshua, we must have that deep foundation laid before we enter into spiritual warfare. We fight from victory to victory on this great truth.

Grace demands that God does it all. We are the recipients of His favor by faith.

The soldier who has this foundational principle built into his life will:

☐ Be confident in Christ's victory over Satan.

☐ Be under the authority of the Christ and therefore will have authority over Satan.

☐ Stand still and wait on God's instructions.

☐ Place more emphasis on prayer than he does on programs.

☐ Seek to rescue those lost in Satan's kingdom

☐ Lay claim to their inheritance in Christ.

5. *"You shall hold your peace."* **The soldier ceases from his own strength to enter into the victory of God's rest.**

The phrase *"You shall hold your peace"* can also be translated *to remain quiet or silent.* It pictures God amplifying His grace in which the work of salvation is His alone. It is not the soldier offering to help God with his feeble weapons or speaking up and giving God a battle strategy. God does it all. The soldier does not lift one finger on his own behalf to save himself. He stands still and sees with the eye of faith God's so great salvation.

Joshua will indeed fight with all his might in the second battle as **the Lord fights with him** against Amalek. However, in this foundational battle at the Red Sea, **the Lord fights for him**.

Every fiber of our flesh will struggle against the principle of grace alone. We feel that we must do something to help God save us. Consider the great Gospel truth of Romans 4:

> *Now to him who works, the wages are not counted as grace but as debt.* ***But to him who does not work*** *but believes on Him who justifies the ungodly, his faith is accounted for righteousness.* (Romans 4:45, emphasis mine)

If Joshua had not learned this principle of resting in silence before God, he would not have been able to obey God with His unusual instructions at Jericho to march around the city in silence for six days. Joshua had learned to wait before God and receive God's wisdom before he battled Jericho. Joshua by faith obeyed and had seen the salvation of the Lord before the shout of victory on the seventh day when the walls of Jericho fell.

Our human nature wants to do something to earn salvation. We attempt to "establish our own righteousness." Imagine saying to a drowning man, "Stay still; don't fight!" But that is exactly what he needs to hear. Until he stops fighting and flailing, it is nearly impossible to rescue him. That's true for us also. Until we stop fighting God and stop trying to save ourselves, we will never be able to be saved by Jesus.

Until we stop fighting God and stop trying to save ourselves,
we will never be able to be saved by Jesus.

In one of his books, Watchman Nee told the story of a lifeguard saving a drowning man. At first, the man panicked and wildly beat the water with his arms and legs. The lifeguard did nothing. He simply stood on the shore and watched the man grow weaker and weaker. When it seemed that the man had no strength left at all, the lifeguard went to his rescue.

Watchman Nee asked the lifeguard why he waited so long to save the man. I have never forgotten the answer: *"The best time to save a drowning man is when he stops trying to save himself."* That's exactly what Paul said in Romans 5:6. *"For when we were still without strength, in due time Christ died for the ungodly."*

31

Like the drowning man, you and I struggle to save ourselves. Surely there is something we can do to earn salvation. But there is not. Christianity is not a self-help program to make you better. It is a rescue plan designed to save you. Man's best attempts at religion tell him to "do." Christianity proclaims, "Done." It is only by the finished work of Christ on the Cross that we can be saved. Notice the common elements in entering into God's rest of salvation:

- Stand still (Exodus 14:13)
- Hold your peace (Exodus 14:14)
- Cease from your own works (Hebrews 4:10)
- Without strength to save yourself (Romans 5:6)
- Not according to our works (Romans 4:2)

Once the foundation of faith is laid in our life, God builds on that same principle of faith as we live the Christian life. We go forward and fight, but we do not fight in our own strength.[3]

The soldier never forgets his salvation was by grace through faith. All future battles build on the principles learned in Christ's finished work on our behalf.

> *The soldier never forgets his salvation was by grace through faith. All future battles build on the principles learned in Christ finished work in our behalf.*

Summation of the Soldier's Foundation Battle

God can do more through us in one day as we rely on His power than we can do in fifty years of self-effort. This should invigorate our prayer life, as we realize that God can work if we just believe Him.

- ☐ We must first stand still, ceasing from our own works.

- ☐ We must believe in Christ's salvation victory on our behalf.

- ☐ We must not be afraid; we must not rely on self-efforts, but trust in God's Spirit and leadership.

- ☐ We must stand still on that which God has already established as His pattern and finished work.

- ☐ We do not fight for victory, but we enter into that rest of the victory that has already been won by Jesus. Then we fight from the victory that Jesus has already won.

---

[3] For a fuller explanation of this principle, see Truman Herring, *God's Greater Purpose in Christ.*

- The faith-rest life is able to praise God for tomorrow's victory today and is able to praise God for victory before the actual battle.

- When we cease from our own works, we will see God do more in a moment than we could ever do.

- We must stand still, believing that the battle is not ours but God's.

 **Application**

God's battle plan at the Rea Sea is the pattern for our salvation. When we are awakened by the Gospel and the Holy Spirit to our helpless lost state, we are also to understand that the Lord Jesus has done for us what we could not do for ourselves.

1. *"Fear not"* is the attitude of faith in salvation.
2. *"Stand still"* is the position of ceasing from our own works to enter into the finished work of Christ.
3. *"See the salvation of the Lord"* is the proper object of faith in salvation that the Lord Jesus has provided by His righteous life, His death on the cross, and His victory over death by His resurrection.
4. *"The Lord shall fight for you"* is the promise of salvation that Jesus alone is God's representative man as the "Second Man" and "The Last Adam" who has defeated sin and Satan for us.
5. *"You shall hold your peace"* is the repentant lost sinner having no faith in himself, transferring his trust instead to the finished work of Christ for salvation.

Do Not Lift One Finger

There is spiritual warfare when we present the Gospel, whether it is one-on-one evangelism or preaching to a crowd. Satan does not stand by idle as we seek to rescue people from bondage. What God said to Paul at his conversion is our mission as well: *"to open their eyes, in order to turn them from darkness to light, and from the power of Satan to God, that they may receive forgiveness of sins"* (Acts 26:18). The Gospel is first hidden from the lost by Satan, who blinds the eyes of those who do not believe (2 Corinthians 4:4).

We are told that the natural mind cannot comprehend the things of God and that His Spirit must reveal them to us (1 Corinthians 2:14).

I was in South Carolina and had the privilege of meeting with a woman who was under deep conviction of her need for Christ by the Holy Spirit. I shared the Gospel and Christ's finished work on her behalf and still she was in a struggle just to trust Christ. In an attempt to find her stumbling block to grace, I asked her to tell me in her own words what she must do to be saved.

She responded, "Before I can be saved, I must quit my job as a waitress at the restaurant." I asked her where she got that idea. Apparently, another preacher had told her that because she served alcohol with the meals the customers ordered, repentance would require her to quit her job before trusting Christ. I am amazed at the ideas people have about the requirements of salvation. In her mind, she had turned "repent and believe the Gospel" into a self-righteous work that kept her from Christ.

I told her she misunderstood the Gospel. As I sat in my armchair, without moving my hand, I lifted just my little finger slightly. I asked her if she could do what I had done and lift her little finger. She did. I asked her how much effort it took to lift her little finger. She responded that it took almost no effort at all.

I then explained that even lifting one little finger to save yourself must be rejected. "If you have to get out of your chair to do anything in order to be saved, then you have the wrong object of your faith. Jesus cried from the cross, 'It is Finished.'" I said, "All you can do is to trust Jesus now where you sit in your chair without lifting one finger."

In that moment she saw it. God opened her eyes to the truth of *"by grace alone through faith alone in Christ alone"* and the burden of her soul was lifted. She understood the Gospel and *"ceased from her own works to enter God rest of salvation."*[4]

Write below a statement in this section that spoke to you.

---

[4] *"Repent and believe"* is the change of mind from *self-works* to *faith in the finished work of Christ alone.* The good works that follow salvation are the fruits of repentance that prove a change of heart in salvation.

Introduction

The second battle that Joshua experienced under the tutelage of Moses happened in Exodus 17. It built on the principles of the battle at the Red Sea—but took both Joshua and Israel to a deeper level.

In the first battle, *the Lord fought for them,* and they stood still and saw the salvation of the Lord. In this second battle, *the Lord fought with them* as Joshua and Israel engaged in hand-to-hand combat in the valley while Moses held up the Rod of God on the hilltop.

God is not required to do today exactly what He did yesterday. He is the Creator, and as such, His creativity is boundless. There are numerous lessons for us to learn, and numerous ways for God to teach us those lessons.

> *There are numerous lessons for us to learn,*
> *and numerous ways for God to teach us those lessons.*

His character never changes. But the ways He works in our lives are boundless.

The foundational battle at the Red Sea pictures for us what Christ has done for us in salvation, delivering us from the penalty of sin. Christ alone lived the perfect and righteous life. Christ alone presented Himself to God as the Lamb of God who takes away the sin of the world. Christ alone defeated Satan and death by His death and resurrection.

In this second battle, we see a picture of what happens to us after salvation. We find ourselves at war with the world, the flesh, and the Devil. This battle is a great picture of the sanctification process that occurs in the life of each believer, in which the flesh and our new nature in Christ fights against each other.

The flesh and the Spirit are at war with each other. We see this principle clearly in the New Testament: *For the flesh wars against the Spirit, and the Spirit against the flesh: and these are contrary the one to the other: so that you cannot do the things that you would* (Galatians 5:17).

Unlike the first battle in which Moses and Joshua stood still and trusted God, the second battle is a fight that requires their obedience. They must prevail by the means of grace that God has given as pictured by Moses interceding and Joshua fighting.

Interceding and fighting. They sound contradictory. But they are not. Both are equally important in winning the battle.

Interceding and fighting. They sound contradictory. But they are not.
Both are equally important in winning the battle.

First, it would be helpful to read the historical account of the attack of Amalek against Israel as they journeyed in the wilderness in Exodus 17:8–16.

> *Now Amalek came and fought with Israel in Rephidim. And Moses said to Joshua, "Choose some men and go out, fight with Amalek. Tomorrow I will stand on the top of the hill with the rod of God in my hand." So Joshua did as Moses said to him, and fought with Amalek. And Moses, Aaron, and Hur went up to the top of the hill. And so it was, when Moses held up his hand, that Israel prevailed; and when he let down his hand, Amalek prevailed. But Moses' hands became heavy; so they took a stone and put it under him, and he sat on it. And Aaron and Hur supported his hands, one on one side, and the other on the other side; and his hands were steady until the going down of the sun. So Joshua defeated Amalek and his people with the edge of the sword.*
>
> *Then the LORD said to Moses, "Write this for a memorial in the book and recount it in the hearing of Joshua, that I will utterly blot out the remembrance of Amalek from under heaven." And Moses built an altar and called its name, The-LORD-Is-My-Banner; for he said, "Because the LORD has sworn: the LORD will have war with Amalek from generation to generation."*

Joshua learns that there are two realms in which every battle is fought. One is the physical realm, in which the soldier battles in hand-to-hand combat. The other is the spiritual realm, in which intercession, prayer, and dependence upon God are seen as the turning point in the battle. Remember verse 11? *And so it was, when Moses held up his hand, that Israel prevailed; and when he let down his hand, Amalek prevailed.*

What was the reason Israel prevailed? Deep, intercessory prayer. And what was the reason Israel failed? Lack of prayer. Let me highlight that so you won't miss it: Prayer will be the reason —the only reason—we succeed. And a failure to pray will be the single reason we fail.

The victory did not turn on the numbers of soldiers or their skill but upon the power of **God their Banner**. The Hebrew phrase is *"Jehovah Nissi."* Let's take a look at the background of that name.

The battle was an unusual one—dependent not on warfare, strategy, or ammunition. The strange way in which the battle was won left no doubt as to who was responsible for the victory. It was Jehovah God, the great *I Am*. Only as the Rod of God was held high did Israel prevail. The battle was not won by military might or superior battle plans. It was won by the power of God. As 1 Samuel 17:47 says, *The battle is the Lord's.*

What a shocking development. Israel had never seen anything like this. God came through —and in recognition of God's deliverance, they *named the place.* They named it *Jehovah Nissi.* It is a combination of Jehovah (the personal *"I Am"* name for God revealed to Moses in Exodus 3:14) and the word for *"banner."* They wanted future generations to remember *this was the place God fought for us and delivered us because we looked to Him.*

A banner was a *flag*—an advertisement, if you will—of whom the army belonged to. They were saying, *"We belong to Jehovah. We trust in Him."* It was a reminder. And no one needed reminding more than Israel. They were quick to forget. The banner would remind them. Their banner must be held high for Israel to see and trust in. This was an important principle for Joshua to learn, as he faced many battles in the conquest of the Promised Land.

This battle reinforced the spiritual strategy that was necessary for future victories like Jericho. God was their deliverer, and they must look wholly to Him. By the way . . . who are you looking to for deliverance? Your spouse? Your boss? Your skill? There's only One who deserves our look of trust. It is Jehovah Nissi!

Important Connecting Links in the Battle with Amalek

Before we look closer at this second battle with Joshua against Amalek, we must see several important events in Exodus 17:1–7 that are linked with this battle. Before the crisis of war in verses 8–16, Israel experienced a crisis of a lack of drinkable water. In both crises, God expected His people to trust Him for deliverance. In each crisis, Christ will be seen in shadow and type.

He died that we drink the Living Water and live eternally. He was resurrected from the dead and forever intercedes for us that we might overcome in this life as we battle the flesh.

Exodus 17 begins with God's divine leadership. The supernatural pillar of cloud by day and fire by night led Israel to Rephidim where there was no water. Just as God led them to the Red Sea, He now led them to a waterless place. He was putting Israel in a place where they again had to trust Him.

When God leads us to a crisis, He refines. He grows us by causing us to turn to Him and trust Him, perhaps in ways we've never had to trust before.

> *When God leads us to a crisis, He refines. He grows us by causing us to turn to Him and trust Him, perhaps in ways we've never had to trust before.*

What did Israel do? Instead of trusting, they complained. They argued. They accused.

"Why is it you have brought us up out of Egypt, to kill us and our children and our livestock with thirst?" The eye of faith would have believed God's promise that they were going to reign in the Promised Land, but they were weary with thirst and did not trust God.

In this setting, Moses cries out to God for deliverance, and God again is gracious to His complaining people.

> *And the LORD said to Moses, "Go on before the people, and take with you some of the elders of Israel. Also take in your hand your rod with which you struck the river, and go. Behold, I will stand before you there on the rock in Horeb; and you shall strike the rock, and water will come out of it, that the people may drink."* (Exodus 17:5–6)

A causal reading of this passage does not tell the whole story. But when you interpret Scripture *with Scripture* (a great principle to employ when you study the Bible), you see so much more. Who could see Christ in a **rod**, a **rock**, and **water** in this passage? Aided by God's own commentary on this event in 1 Corinthians 10:3–4, we learn that the rock that was struck and gave water was Christ: *All ate the same spiritual food, and all drank the same spiritual drink. For they drank of that spiritual Rock that followed them, and that Rock was Christ.*

Consider the key elements in Exodus 17:5–6:

The Rod

The rod was once the rod of Moses that was cast down and became a serpent, but when Moses picked it up by God's instruction, it became the Rod of God. It was a symbol of Moses' leadership, but really it was a greater symbol of God's leadership of the people. With that Rod, Moses struck the Nile and it became blood. He raised that Rod and the judgment of God in

38

the form of plagues fell on Egypt. He raised that Rod and the waters parted. Israel went across the Red Sea on dry land. That Rod spoke of God's judgment and of Israel's deliverance.

Strike the Rock

That Rod of judgment struck Christ the Rock. Here again is one of the many pictures of Christ in our salvation. On the Cross, Christ was struck by the Rod of God's holy judgment against sin. From Him would flow the Living Water of eternal life. We could not know God's mercy if Christ had not been struck by God's judgment for our sins.

Seven hundred years before Jesus was crucified, Isaiah saw Messiah struck by God's judgment:

> *Surely He has borne our griefs, And carried our sorrows; yet we esteemed Him stricken, smitten by God, and afflicted. And the LORD has laid on Him the iniquity of us all.* (Isaiah 53:4, 6)

Water Shall Come Out of It and the People Will Drink

Few things reveal our human weakness and need like thirst. Because Christ was struck with the judgment of sin, we who believe in Christ drink and are satisfied.

Jesus said to the thirsty sinner at the well of Samaria, *"If you drink this water you will thirst again, but whoever drinks of the water that I shall give him will never thirst again"* (John 4:13–14). He provides the living water that every man and woman search for.

He provides the living water that every man and women search for.

Jesus again used the analogy of water when He said,

> *"If anyone thirsts, let him come to Me and drink. He who believes in Me, as the Scripture has said, out of his heart will flow rivers of living water." But this He spoke concerning the Spirit, whom those believing in Him would receive; for the Holy Spirit was not yet given, because Jesus was not yet glorified.* (John 7:37–39)

Notice that the water came after the Rock was struck with the Rod. In like manner, before we can receive the Holy Spirit, Jesus had to first die for our sins, rise the third day, ascend to heaven to receive glory, and sit down on His throne in heaven. It was then that He would pour forth the Holy Spirit on those who believed.

Rock Struck Twice

Before we look closer at the battle with Amalek, it is important that we follow the theme of the Rock of Christ that was struck with God's judgment for our sins.

In Numbers 20, we see a new generation in Israel. Nearly forty years later, they still have the same sin nature of their fathers. They complained to Moses about where God had led them and their need for water. Again, God was gracious and gave them water from the Rock. However, God intended to show the foundation of our provision in Christ who was struck just once in judgment for our sins.

The pattern of God was first He would strike the Rock (Christ) once and for all for sin. Then Christ's ministry as a pleasing sacrifice would be final and complete.

From that moment, the ministry of Christ in heaven as our intercessor became the pattern, where we speak to the Rock in heaven through prayer. We now come boldly to the Throne of Grace through Christ.

> Then the LORD spoke to Moses, saying, "Take the rod; you and your brother Aaron gather the congregation together. **Speak to the rock** before their eyes, and it will yield its water; thus you shall bring water for them out of the rock, and give drink to the congregation and their animals." So Moses took the rod from before the LORD as He commanded him. (Numbers 20:7–9, emphasis mine)

Here God said, "Speak to the Rock." He did not say "Strike the Rock." The rock had already been struck once—and that was enough. But the murmuring people drove Moses to complete frustration, and in anger, he struck the rock—not once, but twice. God considered this act such a violation of the message and type of Christ that He chastened Moses, telling him he would never step foot in the Promised Land.

> *God considered this act such a violation of the message and type of Christ that He punished Moses, telling him he would never step foot in the Promisd Land.*

> So Moses took the rod from before the LORD as He commanded him. And Moses and Aaron gathered the assembly together before the rock; and he said to them, "Hear now, you rebels! Must we bring water for you out of this rock?" Then Moses lifted his hand and struck the rock twice with his rod; and water came out abundantly, and the congregation and their animals drank. Then the LORD spoke to Moses and Aaron, "Because you did not believe Me, to hallow Me in the eyes of the children of Israel, therefore you shall not bring this assembly into the land which I have given them." (Numbers 20:9–12)

That's powerful discipline. Why? What warranted it?

Previously, God made clear to Moses that He had a purpose and pattern in all that He instructed him to do. One reason was that the pattern and shadow on earth revealed God's purpose in heaven.

The high priest (and all the objects in the temple) serve as the copy and shadow of the heavenly things, as Moses was divinely instructed when he was about to make the tabernacle. *For He said, "**See that you make all things according to the pattern shown you** on the mountain." But now He has obtained a more excellent ministry, inasmuch as He is also Mediator of a better covenant, which was established on better promises.* (Hebrews 8:5–6, emphasis mine)

The ministry of Jesus in heaven as our High Priest must be distinct from His ministry on earth as our Sacrifice. This is pointed out in Hebrews clearly. Christ would die **once and for all** for our sins on earth and then enter His high priestly ministry in heaven for us.

- *For this He did **once** for all when He offered up Himself* (Hebrews 7:27, emphasis mine).
- But with His own blood He entered the Most Holy Place **once** for all, having obtained eternal redemption (Hebrews 9:12, emphasis mine).
- ***Once** at the end of the ages, He has appeared to put away sin by the sacrifice of Himself* (Hebrews 9:27, emphasis mine).
- *So Christ was offered **once** to bear the sins of many* (Hebrews 9:28, emphasis mine).
- *By that will we have been sanctified through the offering of the body of Jesus Christ **once** for all* (Hebrews 10:10, emphasis mine).

This valuable lesson learned from Moses' failure was not to be lost on Joshua. He was to follow God's instructions, not his own, if he was to overcome an enemy much stronger than Israel.

This valuable lesson learned from Moses' failure was not to be lost on Joshua.
He was to follow God's instructions, not his own,
if he was to overcome an enemy much stronger than Israel.

We will see later that Joshua, just like his mentor Moses, will deviate from God's pattern and suffer defeat on the battlefield in Canaan.

The Battle with Our Flesh

Now Amalek came and fought with Israel in Rephidim (Exodus 17:8).

The second battle came when Amalek attacked Israel. In this instance, the plan of God was not for Israel to stand still. Here they were to engage the enemy in hand-to-hand combat. But the principle would not be forgotten: the battle is not won by might or the power of man but *"by My Spirit,"* says the Lord.

There are several keys here for us to understand our spiritual battle as well.

There are four things we should notice as to the origin of this battle: *first, the significance of who attacked; second, why they attacked; third, when they attacked, and finally how they attacked.*

1. **First, who attacked?**

   The origin of Amalek points to the battle we have with our flesh. Amalek was the grandson of Esau. Esau is seen in Scripture as one who sold his birthright to Jacob for a single meal (Genesis 25:29–34). The divine commentary on Esau is given in Hebrews 12:16–17:

   … Lest there be any fornicator or profane person like Esau, who for one morsel of food sold his birthright. For you know that afterward, when he wanted to inherit the blessing, he was rejected, for he found no place for repentance, though he sought it diligently with tears.

   In despising his birthright, he rejected the promise God made to Abraham that the seed of the Messiah would come through his lineage.

2. **Why would Amalek attack Israel?**

   Following the bitter spirit of Esau, his descendants, the Amalekites, made themselves continual enemies of Israel. From this vantage point, we see that the flesh also makes war with the believer in Christ every day. The reason Amalek hated Israel is seen in Deuteronomy 25:18 where it is said that *he did not fear God.*

3. **When did Amalek attack Israel?**

   Amalek attacked Israel just after the Rod struck the Rock and water came forth to the thirsty Hebrews. This is the pattern with us as well. After we believe in Christ and receive the Holy Spirit, the flesh is stirred up against us.

   I say then: Walk in the Spirit, and you shall not fulfill the lust of the flesh. For the flesh lusts against the Spirit, and the Spirit against the flesh; and these are contrary to one another. (Galatians 5:16–17)

   A. W. Pink has written some very wise words in this regard:

   It is not until the Christian has been made partaker of the Divine nature (2 Pet. 1:4) that the inward conflict begins…. It is striking to note that it was not Israel who attacked Amalek, but Amalek that attacked Israel. The new nature in the believer

42

delights to feed upon the Word, to commune with God, and be engaged with spiritual things. But the flesh will not let him live in peace."[5]

> *"The new nature in the believer delights to feed upon the Word, to commune with God, and be engaged with spiritual things. But the flesh will not let him live in peace."*

Paul describes his war with his flesh in Romans 7:17–25 and declares that Jesus Christ is the only One who can deliver him from the power of the flesh.

> *But now, it is no longer I who do it, but sin that dwells in me. For I know that in me (that is, in my flesh) nothing good dwells; for to will is present with me, but how to perform what is good I do not find. For the good that I will to do, I do not do; but the evil I will not to do, that I practice. Now if I do what I will not to do, it is no longer I who do it, but sin that dwells in me. I find then a law, that evil is present with me, the one who wills to do good. For I delight in the law of God according to the inward man. But I see another law in my members, warring against the law of my mind, and bringing me into captivity to the law of sin which is in my members. O wretched man that I am! Who will deliver me from this body of death? I thank God—through Jesus Christ our Lord! (Romans 7:17–24)*

One evidence that we have been saved and indwelt and empowered with the Holy Spirit is the reality of our daily battle with the flesh and our dependence upon God and the means of grace to fight sin.

4. How did Amalek attack?

Amalek attacked Israel at their weakest point—when they were tired and weary. This has always been the strategy of Satan: to find the weak area in our flesh where we have yielded to some temptation of sin. It is where we have grieved the Spirit that the flesh is able to make its greatest inroads.

> *This has always been the strategy of Satan: to find the weak area in our flesh where we have yielded to some temptation of sin. It is where we have grieved the Spirit that the flesh is able to make its greatest inroads.*

> *Remember what Amalek did to you on the way as you were coming out of Egypt, how he met you on the way and attacked your rear ranks, all the stragglers at your rear, when you were tired and weary; and he did not fear God (Deuteronomy 25:17).*

---

[5] Pink, A.W. (1964). Gleanings in Joshua . Chicago: Moody Press

God declared war on Amalek forever. The same is true of our flesh. The soldier of Christ soon discovers that the weakest points in his flesh give place to Satan for his attacks. Knowing his greatest enemy is his own flesh, he must learn to battle his flesh by yielding to the Holy Spirit on a daily basis.

We will pick up the story of the battle with Amalek in the next chapter.

 **Application**

Have you recognized the spiritual battle within you, between the flesh and the new nature in Christ? Read Romans 7:17–24 and write out a short prayer below:

Introduction

In the previous chapter, we saw the background behind Amalek's attack on Israel. Let's move on in our understanding of this passage. God does something entirely different than He did at the Red Sea. There, He fought *for* Israel. Here, He fights on the battlefield *with* Israel.

The Two Battlefields for the Soldier

And Moses said to Joshua, "Choose us some men and go out, fight with Amalek. Tomorrow I will stand on the top of the hill with the rod of God in my hand." And so it was, when Moses held up his hand, that Israel prevailed; and when he let down his hand, Amalek prevailed (Exodus 17:9, 11).

Joshua and his inexperienced army fought in hand-to-hand combat with Amalek's experienced army on the battlefield. This battle was not like the battle at the Red Sea, where the Lord fought for Israel and completely destroyed Pharaoh's army. In this battle, Joshua would have to depend on the Lord to strengthen him and fight with him.

As Joshua engaged Amalek, he had success. But in the middle of the battle, Amalek began to cut down Joshua's men. They were dying before Joshua's eyes. It was here that Joshua and Israel learned that there was a direct correlation between Moses holding high the Rod of God and victory.

When Moses arms grew tired and he had no strength left to hold up the Rod of God, he watched as his people began to die by Amalek's sword. Can you imagine the burden Moses must have carried knowing that many lives were dependent on his strength to intercede for Israel?

It becomes obvious that the victory did not turn on the numbers of soldiers or their skill, but upon *Jehovah Nissi*, their banner that must be held high for Israel to see and trust in. This was an important principle for Joshua to learn, as he would face many battles in the conquest of the

Promised Land. This battle would reinforce the spiritual strategy that was necessary for future victories, like at Jericho.

The first battle Israel faced pictured salvation, where Israel stood still and saw God's gracious deliverance. This second battle is more like sanctification, where we are daily attacked by the world, the flesh, and the Devil. In this battle, we are to fight the good fight of faith and to use all the means of grace that a good soldier has been given by God. Yet the battle is a blend and balance of discipline and obedience on the battlefield and dependence upon prayer and intercession.

Prayer and Intercession Decide the Outcome on the Battlefield

But Moses' hands became heavy; so they took a stone and put it under him, and he sat on it. And Aaron and Hur supported his hands, one on one side, and the other on the other side; and his hands were steady until the going down of the sun. So Joshua defeated Amalek and his people with the edge of the sword. (Exodus 17:12–13)

Most commentators see Moses' role in this battle as an intercessor, praying for his people in battle. As such, Moses foreshadows the high priestly ministry of Jesus interceding for us.

Warren Wiersbe was an American pastor, a Bible teacher, and a prolific writer. His comment on this passage is filled with insight:

How did Israel overcome the enemy? They had an intercessor on the mountain and a commander in the valley! Moses' role on the mountain illustrates the intercessory work of Christ, and Joshua with his sword illustrates the Spirit of God using the Word of God against the enemy (Heb. 4:12 and Eph. 6:17–18). Of course, Moses is an imperfect picture of Christ and His intercessory work, since our Lord never wearies and needs no assistance (Heb. 4:16; 9:24). Paul says that believers can "help together by prayer" (2 Cor. 1:11), which is what Aaron and Hur did.[6]

"Believers can 'help together by prayer,' which is what Aaron and Hur did."

Though the church holds up our hands in prayer, it is ultimately the intercession of the One who is greater than Moses, who never grows weary, and holds up his Rod as our Advocate and High Priest, and who ever lives to make intercession for us.

What Moses was to Joshua in this battle, the Lord Jesus is to us as we battle the world, the flesh, and the Devil. Isaiah 53 describes our Lord Jesus going to a hill called Calvary **to make**

---
[6] Wiersbe, W. W. (1993). *Wiersbe's Expository Outlines on the Old Testament* (Ex 17:1–7). Wheaton, IL: Victor Books.

intercession for us on the Cross. Jesus cried, *"Father, forgive them."* There is a beautiful line in a wonderful Christian song that says, *"When He was on the cross, I was on His mind."* As we fight our self-life and Satan, it brings great comfort to know that in His agony, He was praying for us. We prevail because Jesus made intercession for **us on the Cross, before the Cross, and after the Cross.**

> *Yet it pleased the LORD to bruise Him; He has put Him to grief. When You make His soul an offering for sin, He shall see His seed, He shall prolong His days, and the pleasure of the LORD shall prosper in His hand. He shall see the labor of His soul, and be satisfied. By His knowledge My righteous Servant shall justify many, for He shall bear their iniquities. Therefore I will divide Him a portion with the great, and He shall divide the spoil with the strong, because He poured out His soul unto death, and He was numbered with the transgressors, and He bore the sin of many, **and made intercession for the transgressors.*** (Isaiah 53:10–12, emphasis mine)

Unlike Moses whose hands grew weary, our Lord never grows weary and never stops interceding for us. His intercession is seen **before** He went to the Cross in John 17:

> *I pray for them. I do not pray for the world but for those whom You have given Me, for they are Yours…. Now I am no longer in the world, but these are in the world, and I come to You. Holy Father, keep through Your name those whom You have given Me, that they may be one…. I have given them Your word; and the world has hated them because they are not of the world, just as I am not of the world. I do not pray that You should take them out of the world, but that You should keep them from the evil one…. As You sent Me into the world, I also have sent them into the world. I do not pray for these alone, but also for those who will believe in Me through their word.* (John 17:9, 11, 14, 18, 20)

Jesus continually makes intercession for us **after the Cross**. As we battle our flesh and Satan on earth, Jesus is in heaven ever living to make intercession for us.

> *Who shall bring a charge against God's elect? It is God who justifies. Who is he who condemns? It is Christ who died, and furthermore is also risen, who is even at the right hand of God, who also makes intercession for us.* (Romans 8:33–34)

> *Therefore He is also able to save to the uttermost those who come to God through Him, since He always lives to make intercession for them.* (Hebrews 7:25)

Jesus is praying for us. He's praying for you. Specifically. But have you ever thought to ask, "What is He praying for me about?" Take some time and read Jesus' prayer for His followers, as recorded in John 17. This is the true "Lord's Prayer." [7]

---

[7] The *"Lord's Prayer"* that you are probably thinking about, as recorded in Luke 11, is more accurately *"The Disciples' Prayer."* They asked Him to teach them to pray, and Luke 11:2–4 is what He taught **them** to pray. John 17 is what He actually prayed **for them and for us.**

Jesus' Prayer for His Disciples – and for Us – John 17:1-26	
What Did Jesus Pray for Us?	**Why Is That Important?**

Like Joshua, we must learn that we do not prevail by our strength alone. We must buffet the body and bring it under control. We must be disciplined and say no to the flesh and yes to the indwelling Spirit. We must obey God and use the means of grace God has given us to strengthen us in battle. However, we must have our eyes fixed on Christ, depending on Him and remembering His words, *"Without Me you can do nothing"* (John 15:5).

The soldier who is indwelt with the Spirit of God is compelled from within to pray and to become an intercessor in this battle on earth (Romans 8:26–27). The Holy Spirit takes the burden of heaven and places it on the heart of the believer on earth to become part of God's incredible circle of intercession to accomplish God's will on earth.

> *Likewise, the Spirit also helps in our weaknesses. For we do not know what we should pray for as we ought, but the Spirit Himself makes intercession for us with groanings which cannot be uttered. Now He who searches the hearts knows what the mind of the Spirit is, because He makes intercession for the saints according to the will of God.* (Romans 8:26–27)

Prayer and intercession make the difference. This is seen throughout the Bible. The apostle Paul in Acts 27 was a Roman prisoner sailing to Rome. God showed him the disaster that would befall them all on their voyage: *"Men, I perceive that this voyage will end with disaster and much loss, not only of the cargo and ship, but also our lives"* (Acts 27:10). After many days in a hurricane-like storm, all hope for survival was lost. However, Paul prayed. Like Moses, he held up his hands in intercession until God granted his request that no lives would be lost.

> *"And now I urge you to take heart, for there will be no loss of life among you, but only of the ship. For there stood by me this night an angel of the God to whom I belong and whom I serve, saying, 'Do not be afraid, Paul; you must be brought before Caesar; and indeed God has granted you all those who sail with you.'"* (Acts 27:22–24)

Notice closely that something major changed through Paul's intercession. In the beginning, there was going to be loss of life. But God granted Paul's request, and everyone was saved. What a powerful example and encouragement for us to make a difference through prayer!

What a powerful example and encouragement for us
to make a difference through prayer!

Leaders Should Be Supported in the Work of God

Leaders need help. Pastors are not omnipotent. They cannot do everything. Aaron and Hur came alongside Moses at a time when he was weak and needed their help and encouragement.

But Moses' hands became heavy; so they took a stone and put it under him, and he sat on it. And Aaron and Hur supported his hands, one on one side, and the other on the other side; and his hands were steady until the going down of the sun. So Joshua defeated Amalek and his people with the edge of the sword. (Exodus 17:12–13)

Don't believe the lie that "spiritual people" never get tired in prayer. Many Christian leaders kneel by their beds in prayer, only to wake up two hours later. Becoming weary in prayer is a reality in ministry. Even though we are doing our part in the work of God, we get tired, weary, and discouraged at times. Moses was not disobedient to God, for he stood in faith. But he was human, and therefore limited in strength.

Moses knew that ministry was hard. He was carrying his people on his heart, even though they often murmured and complained. More than once, he had to intercede for them before God, that God might pardon them and not destroy them. Once the burden was so heavy that God took some of the Spirit on Moses and placed it on seventy elders who were to carry the burden with him.

Here we see the wisdom of God in giving Moses, Aaron, and Hur to be supporters in this battle with Amalek. They were there to hold up Moses' hands when he reached his human limitation. Aaron and Hur were needed if Israel was to prevail. God not only accepted the fact that others helped in this battle, He ordained it.

This is true of us as well in the ministry of the Church. God has not made us **independent** in His mission on earth. We are **interdependent** in the body of Christ. God made the church such that no one person has all the gifts and enabling of the Holy Spirit to accomplish His mission. We are in this fight together.

*God has not made us **independent** in His mission on earth. We are **interdependent** in the body of Christ. God made the church such that no one person has all the gifts and enabling of the Holy Spirit to accomplish His mission. We are in this fight together.*

49

Jesus sent the disciples out two by two. They needed each other's support. Paul had companions with him on his missionary journeys, because, like Moses, he needed his hands held up as well. Timothy and Epaphroditus "held up Paul's hands" in Philippians 2.

Moses was not alone on the hill … and Joshua was not alone in the valley. Both were leaders with a different assignment in the battle. And God gave them others to help in their mission.

Let me highlight two insights about prayer at this point.

1. *"Holding up hands"* was a figurative description of Moses' physical posture. The power wasn't in the posture, but in the prayer.

2. Nevertheless, posture in prayer is important. Kneeling communicates to us and to God our submission to Him. *"Raising up holy hands"* shows both our desperation and dependence. We bring nothing to the table but our plea for His help.

Have you ever tried to hold your hands over your head for even a few minutes? Not so easy. But imagine that the lives of friends and family are dependent on those hands staying raised. Moses held up his hands, knowing there was a relationship between holding up his hands and victory for Israel. Can you imagine the weight of responsibility he must have felt? He started struggling … and that's when his friends showed up. Moses prayed … but Aaron and Hur supported him. Joshua and the troops fought down on the battlefield. But they were not alone. They were supported by spiritual intercession, which was absolutely necessary for Israel's victory.

Soldiers with swords in their hands are no match for iron tanks on the battlefield.

In World War II, Germany prepared to invade Poland. The Polish people were ready. They were experienced warriors with a long history of repelling enemy attacks from barbarian neighbors. And they had a great cavalry. They were well-trained and their horses were among Europe's finest.

When they learned that German forces were advancing, twelve brigades of their finest cavalry were prepared. With swords flashing in the sunlight, the officers sounded the charge, and their horses surged forward with powerful strides. Remember the time frame. This was World War II.

The cavalry galloped into oncoming, newly designed German Panzer tanks. The outcome was predictable—total annihilation! Horsemen with swords attempted to battle iron tanks. They were completely outmatched.

I'm convinced that we, as believers, often expect to take on the enemy of our soul with methods similar to that of galloping on horseback at full speed, heading into the path of an oncoming tank division.[8]

Even worse, we enter our daily activity without so much as a thought that we have an enemy who is on a search-and-destroy mission. Satan seeks to deceive, to distract, and to defeat any attempt by Christians who desire to advance the kingdom of light and the glory of the Prince of Heaven.

Paul warned us that the battle would be fierce. But in Ephesians 6, as he sums up our spiritual armor, he tells us to *pray at all times in the Spirit, with all prayer and supplication. To that end, keep alert with all perseverance, making supplication for all the saints* (Ephesians 6:18).

Prayer isn't preparation for the battle. Prayer *is* the battle.

---

*Prayer isn't preparation for the battle. Prayer **is** the battle.*

In the next chapter, we will take a brief interlude before the third battle to see how God prepared Joshua to become a godly soldier.

Write below a statement in this section that spoke to you.

---

[8] Adapted from Stephen Davey, *Wisdom for the Heart,* www.wisdomonline.org, January 12, 2018.

Introduction

In the previous two chapters, we've seen the background behind Amalek's attack on Israel and the importance of prayer and intercession in the battle. While Moses battled in prayer on top of the mountain, Joshua fought a real and physical fight on the battlefield. In this chapter, we'll focus on the development of Joshua as a true soldier of God before we proceed to the third battle in our series.

The Preparation of Joshua to Become God's Soldier

Are leaders born or made? Well, I've never met a leader who hasn't been born! But the reality is that there is a pattern of development in the life of every man and woman who becomes a leader.[9]

God's purpose is to mature every one of His sons and daughters. As we grow and mature spiritually, we become effective in ministry to others. Some will be given a title of *leader,* but all of us are designed to be spiritual influencers who lead others to Christ and disciple them to maturity.

> *All of us are designed to be spiritual influencers*
> *who lead others to Christ and disciple them to maturity.*

Soldiers are sons and daughters who have matured in their walk with God and have become active in advancing God's kingdom.

John describes this progression of maturity from little children to young men[10] in 1 John 2:12–14, reminding those **children**, who are young in their faith, that their sins are forgiven for

---

[9] I encourage you to read my book, *A Ministry That Pleases God: Learning to Do God's Work God's Way* to learn more about God's plan to take young men and women and mold them into the leaders He wants them to be.

Jesus' sake, and that they are secure in God who loves them as their heavenly Father. John also praises **young men** who have overcome the wicked one, are strong, and the Word of God abides in them.

As God's soldier, Joshua became an overcomer. He grew strong in the Lord and in His Word.

Joshua was not born a soldier. He was born a slave. By faith, He trusted God and became a son, who grew to become a good soldier of the Lord. Let's follow that progression in Joshua's life.

1. Joshua Began as a Slave

Joshua was born as a slave to Pharaoh in Egypt. He grew up in bondage, never experiencing the blessings of freedom and liberty. In his poverty, he had to work to make Pharaoh rich. He experienced the many injustices of slavery and felt the pain of the foreman's whip across his back. He observed the great contrast between the many gods that Egypt worshiped and the one true God of his father Abraham.

He was among those Hebrew slaves who groaned and cried out to God for deliverance. At some point in his life, God revealed to him that he was more than a slave to Pharaoh. He was also a slave to Satan and sin. As such, he had to cry out to God for mercy and forgiveness for his own sins.

> *Then the children of Israel groaned because of the bondage, and they cried out; and their cry came up to God because of the bondage. So God heard their groaning, and God remembered His covenant with Abraham, with Isaac, and with Jacob. And God looked upon the children of Israel, and God acknowledged them.* (Exodus 2:23–25)

Little did Joshua know that when God heard their groaning and remembered His covenant, that God was at work preparing him to become God's soldier who would lead Israel in the conquest of the Promised Land. Israel complained because the circumstances looked bleak. But God was already at work.

> *God was at work preparing him to become God's soldier who would lead Israel in the conquest of the Promised Land. Israel complained because the circumstances looked bleak. But God was already at work.*

The scars that Joshua carried into battle as God's soldier must have continually reminded Joshua of God's mercy and calling in his life. The same is true for us as well.

---

[10] Although John uses the terms *young men* and *sons*, it should be recognized that this principle clearly applies to both men and women

Whatever the sins and scars from our life before Christ may be, God can redeem them. He works all things together for our good and His glory (Romans 8:28).

> *Whatever the sins and scars from our life before Christ may be, God can redeem them. He works all things together for our good and His glory (Romans 8:28).*

Are there things you regret from your life before Christ? Did you participate in things that, if they were to become public, would make you mortified? Are there things you've done that still seem to have a hold on you? My friend, let me give you some good news:

The Bible says you are a new person. The Bible says that whatever happened in the past is in the past: *forgiven and forgotten.* Paul put it this way:

> *If anyone is in Christ, he is a new creation. Old things have passed away. Behold, all things have become new!* (2 Corinthians 5:17)

That IS good news, isn't it? You are forgiven. In God's eyes, you are a completely new person. The past is the past. Don't let it hold you down. Live free as a son or daughter of Jesus!

> *You are forgiven. In God's eyes, you are a completely new person. The past is the past. Don't let it hold you down. Live free as a son or daughter of Jesus!*

A. The soldier prepared for spiritual warfare must never forget he was once a slave.

Joshua was a slave to Pharaoh and cried out to God because of his bondage. We, too, were once under Satan's and sin's bondage in our lost state. We must remember our bondage if we are to have the will to fight the tyranny of Satan and sin.

> *And you He made alive, who were dead in trespasses and sins, in which you once walked according to the course of this world, according to the prince of the power of the air, the spirit who now works in the sons of disobedience, among whom also we all once conducted ourselves in the lusts of our flesh, fulfilling the desires of the flesh and of the mind, and were by nature children of wrath, just as the others.* (Ephesians 2:1–3)

Once you were a slave to sin. Now you are set free by the death of Jesus. Are you living in that freedom? Are you experiencing on a daily basis freedom from fear, stress, condemnation, lies, and accusation? Never forget you were once a slave. But always remember you are now set free.

B. The soldier must never forget his redemption from bondage.

Do you remember the story in Exodus 11–12? It was God's final judgment upon Egypt. The death angel was to visit the land, and he was to bring death to the firstborn of every household in Egypt. However, there was a grace-provision: if God's people would sacrifice a lamb, taking its blood and painting the doorposts of their house with it. When the death angel came to the house, he would see the blood and "pass over" it, sparing the life of the firstborn. The blood of this lamb, known in the future as the Passover Lamb, spared the lives of many.

Joshua was the firstborn of his father's house. He was marked for death and ordained to die. However, by faith in God and His provision in the Passover Lamb, he was redeemed by the blood of the Lamb. He was marked by and purchased by the redemption blood to be God's servant and soldier forever.

God said that *"all the firstborn are Mine"* (Numbers 3:13). Joshua carried with him a consciousness that he belonged to a new, loving master in Jehovah.

> *And thus you shall eat it: with a belt on your waist, your sandals on your feet, and your staff in your hand. So you shall eat it in haste. It is the LORD's Passover. For I will pass through the land of Egypt on that night, and will strike all the firstborn in the land of Egypt, both man and beast; and against all the gods of Egypt I will execute judgment: I am the LORD. Now the blood shall be a sign for you on the houses where you are. And when I see the blood, I will pass over you; and the plague shall not be on you to destroy you when I strike the land of Egypt. 'So this day shall be to you a memorial; and you shall keep it as a feast to the LORD throughout your generations* (Exodus 12:11–14).

We cannot be effective in spiritual warfare against Satan if we do not understand the value that God places on the redemption blood. We must focus on Jesus, *in whom we have redemption through his blood, the forgiveness of sins, according to the riches of his grace* (Ephesians 1:7). We are told in Revelation 12:11 that believers *overcame Satan by the blood of the Lamb.* Like Joshua, we have been bought with a price and we are not our own but have become the Lord's slaves. In Christ, we find both our liberty and authority. It is this authority in Christ that enables us to have victory in spiritual warfare.

> *Or do you not know that your body is the temple of the Holy Spirit who is in you, whom you have from God, and you are not your own? For you were bought at a price; therefore, glorify God in your body and in your spirit, which are God's.* (1 Corinthians 6:19–20)

Joshua was aware that he was redeemed from slavery to Pharaoh both by blood and by power. Joshua had been an eyewitness to the mighty power of God as He directed a plague at each of the gods that Egyptians worshiped. Joshua saw God's power over nature to control frogs, locust, lice, storms, disease, and even the sun. Those displays prepared Joshua to lead Israel to fight God's battles.

Because he had seen God's power to redeem Israel from Pharaoh, Joshua could believe that God's power would work for him at Jericho and the conquest of the mighty nations of Canaan. This man who was once a common slave to Pharaoh would one day stand as God's soldier on the battlefield in Canaan and cry out to God to stop the sun in its tracks until he had destroyed his enemies.

> *So the sun stood still in the midst of heaven, and did not hasten to go down for about a whole day. And there has been no day like that, before it or after it, that the LORD heeded the voice of a man; for the LORD fought for Israel.* (Joshua 10:13–14)

The soldier must never forget the great demonstration of God's power in our redemption. Our focus determines our fate. Are you focusing on the circumstances in front of you, or are you focusing on God's redemptive power? As we grow in grace and study the Scriptures, we discover more and more of the great love, grace, and power that God demonstrated in Christ.

Our focus determines our fate. Are you focusing on the circumstances in front of you, or are you focusing on God's redemptive power? As we grow in grace and study the Scriptures, we discover more and more of the great love, grace, and power that God demonstrated in Christ.

It is our growing understanding in God's great salvation that is the foundation for us to be good soldiers of Jesus Christ.

2. Joshua Grew as a Servant

Part of God's training for Joshua to be a good soldier was to learn many lessons as a servant to God and to Moses.

A. As a servant, Joshua learned the principle of submission.

God personally selected Moses to be His man to lead Israel out of the bondage of Egypt. He had also called Joshua to be the man that would lead Israel in the conquest of

Canaan by war. Moses was to personally mentor, encourage, and command Joshua in his preparation for this God-size assignment.

God commended both Moses and Joshua in their faithfulness as servants to God:

> As the LORD had commanded Moses his servant, so Moses commanded Joshua, and so Joshua did. He left nothing undone of all that the LORD had commanded Moses. (Joshua 11:15)

There were probably times when Joshua wondered about his role as a servant to Moses. A few months dragged on to be forty years in the wilderness. Wandering around the desert got old. Manna became predicable. But Joshua remained faithful.

No one is qualified to lead in God's army that has not first learned to be a faithful follower. One who is submissive to the Lord in his personal walk with God will demonstrate that submissive attitude at home, at church, and at work. Joshua learned that as he served and ministered to Moses, God was preparing him for his future leadership role. God would indeed promote him in His perfect timing.

Jesus was the perfect mentor by example and teaching in preparing His disciples as servants to become good soldiers of Christ. When James and John sought to be exalted above the other disciples, Jesus used that teaching moment to say,

> You know that the rulers of the Gentiles lord it over them, and those who are great exercise authority over them. Yet it shall not be so among you; but whoever desires to become great among you, let him be your servant. And whoever desires to be first among you, let him be your slave—just as the Son of Man did not come to be served, but to serve, and to give His life a ransom for many. (Matthew 20:25–28)

Patrick Morley wrote,

> It is not that the Holy Spirit empowers a person to become more dynamic, eloquent, and persuasive—though all these may possibly come. Rather, it is that the Holy Spirit helps you to become nothing to yourself, you "become less." Not servile, but a servant. Don't ask the Holy Spirit to increase your skill; ask Him to increase Christ.
>
> The servant no longer wants to become a great man of God; he wants to become less. His love for the Lord Jesus becomes such an intense fire that he abandons all desire to be liked, to do a good job, to have a winning way, to be great man of God. He loses interest in who holds first place. He stakes out his claim on last place. His highest aim becomes for Christ to increase, for himself to decrease.[11]

---

[11] Morley, Patrick, *Walking with Christ in the Details of Life* (Nashville: Thomas Nelson Publishers, 1992), p. 128.

B. As a servant, Joshua learned the principle of solitude with God.

Moses learned the importance of quietly waiting on God in solitude and patience. He learned to wait on God to discover more about God's character and will. He had forty years of waiting and learning … but those forty years taught him not to rush ahead of God and attempt to deliver God's people with his own strength. After his burning bush encounter with God on the backside of the desert, he returned in God's power with a shepherd's rod. Moses had learned to wait alone on God.

Moses passed that principle on to Joshua.

When God called Moses to wait before Him on Mt. Sinai for forty days, Moses instructed his servant to sit and wait on the mountain until he returned. *So Moses arose with his assistant Joshua, and Moses went up to the mountain of God* (Exodus 24:13).

Joshua sat alone between Moses, higher up on the mountain, and Aaron and the people down below in the camp. Joshua did not know how long he was to wait. He did not know if Moses would return in a day, a week, forty days, or eighty days. All Joshua knew was that he was to sit and wait and trust God and his leader Moses.

Can you imagine how hard this must have been? A hundred questions must have filled his mind. Yet he remained like a good soldier at his post, following the last command he had received.

God's Word clearly marks the difference between faithful Joshua and the people in the camp who could not wait on God.

> *Now when the people saw that Moses delayed coming down from the mountain, the people gathered together to Aaron, and said to him, "Come, make us gods that shall go before us; for as for this Moses, the man who brought us up out of the land of Egypt, we do not know what has become of him."* (Exodus 32:1)

Aaron quickly capitulated to the temptation. With the encouragement of the sinful people, he made an idol of a golden calf and made false sacrifices to it. Aaron and the people could not wait on God. If Moses had not interceded for the people, God would have destroyed them.

We are given another scene in which we see Joshua's heart to stay in the presence of God where *Moses' servant Joshua, the son of Nun, a young man, did not depart from the tabernacle* (Exodus 33:11). He was a true worshipper who loved to be in the presence of God. Those who know God intimately worship passionately. They don't go "through the motions" in worship; they worship God wholeheartedly, in spirit and in truth.

Those who know God intimately worship passionately. They don't go through the motions; they worship God wholeheartedly, in spirit and in truth.

The disciples noticed how Jesus woke up early to go and be alone with God in prayer. It was watching this example that caused the disciples to ask Jesus, *"Lord, teach us to pray."* Please notice: they didn't ask Jesus how to preach. They didn't request strategic insight about how to grow a church. They saw what was most important and asked, *"Lord, teach us to pray."*

Theologian D. A. Carson says that if you really want to embarrass the average Christian, just ask them to tell you about their private prayer life. Many of us can impress others with our Bible knowledge or our evangelism stories, but our private prayer times are simply embarrassing.

Every servant of God whom God uses has to develop and desire solitude with God. Solitude is used by God to remember our past mercies and spiritual lessons, to evaluate the present, and to gain a vision for the future.

It was this quality of character of waiting on God that would benefit Joshua at Jericho when God would command Israel to march around Jericho for six days in silence before they shouted on the seventh day.

Aaron could not wait. Idolatry resulted. Saul could not wait and was deposed as king. Jesus told the disciples to wait in the Upper Room. They did and they were blessed with the power of the Holy Spirit.

Let me give you a great idea of a Bible study you can do in your own home. Read through the book of Acts and highlight every mention of prayer. You can literally find the church in prayer in every single chapter of Acts. It was *fundamental* to what they did. Here's my concern: what was fundamental for the early church has become supplemental to churches today. The soldier must learn that before he rushes ahead in battle he must sit before God to receive his instructions and power.

Here's my concern: what was fundamental for the early church has become supplemental to churches today.

C. As a servant, Joshua learned the principle of meekness.

God called Moses the meekest man on earth (Numbers 12:3, KJV). Meekness can best be defined as "strength under control." Moses knew who he was and what his gifts were. But more importantly, he knew who God was and that he needed to depend on God completely if he was going to accomplish God's purposes in his generation.

> *Moses knew he was and what his gifts were. But more importantly, he knew who God was and that he needed to depend on God completely if he was going to accomplish God's purposes in his generation.*

However, Moses did not begin his ministry that way. Moses *was learned in all the wisdom of the Egyptians, and was mighty in words and deeds* (Acts 7:22). He accomplished much in Pharaoh's house, and he had a sense of pride in his leadership abilities. He knew that God had chosen him to deliver Israel from Pharaoh's bondage, but he had not yet seen the depths of his own pride and self-dependency. After Moses took his sword and tried to deliver a Hebrew slave, he fled in fear from the wrath of Pharaoh. For the next forty years, God worked to make Moses his meek servant who would indeed lead the Hebrew slaves out of bondage.

God never stops working in our lives. *He who began a good work in you is faithful to complete it* (Philippians 1:6). Whatever you are going through right now, God is using it to make you more like Jesus and using it to prepare you for greater ministry in the days ahead.

Moses knew the difference between attempting to do God's will in his own strength, and humble dependence upon God to accomplish God's will. He became the perfect mentor for Joshua's preparation to become both a humble servant and courageous soldier.

There was a time Moses became aware of a lesson Joshua needed to learn.

> *So Moses went out and told the people the words of the Lord, and he gathered the seventy men of the elders of the people and placed them around the tabernacle. Then the Lord came down in the cloud, and spoke to him, and took of the Spirit that was upon him, and placed the same upon the seventy elders; and it happened, when the Spirit rested upon them, that they prophesied, although they never did so again. But two men had remained in the camp: the name of one was Eldad, and the name of the other Medad. And the Spirit rested upon them. Now they were among those*

listed, but who had not gone out to the tabernacle; yet they prophesied in the camp. And a young man ran and told Moses, and said, "Eldad and Medad are prophesying in the camp."

So Joshua the son of Nun, Moses' assistant, one of his choice men, answered and said, "Moses my lord, forbid them!" Then Moses said to him, "Are you zealous for my sake? Oh, that all the Lord's people were prophets and that the Lord would put His Spirit upon them!" And Moses returned to the camp, he and the elders of Israel. (Numbers 11:24–30)

Moses took this teachable moment in which Joshua's love for and allegiance to Moses stirred up the pride of envy in Joshua. The lesson Joshua needed to learn was that it didn't matter who got the credit as long as God got the glory.

This lesson would not be in vain. Joshua would lead the greatest generation of Israel in the conquest of the Promised Land as God's strong and meek soldier. Under his leadership, all of Israel became soldiers fighting under the one Master and giving the glory to God.

Paul reminds us that we too must walk in humility if we are to be good soldiers of Jesus Christ.

I, therefore, the prisoner of the Lord, beseech you to walk worthy of the calling with which you were called, with all lowliness and gentleness, with longsuffering, bearing with one another in love. (Ephesians 4:1–2)

Paul reminds us that we too must walk in humility
if we are to be good soldiers of Jesus Christ.

One of the greatest lessons we must learn as good soldiers of God is that the power is not in the person but in humility and total dependence upon God. God's power is not limited to one individual but should be manifested through all of God's soldiers in spiritual warfare.

D. As a servant, Joshua learned the principle of faith.

This was a must-learn lesson. Joshua would not be qualified to lead Israel in the conquest of the Promised Land had he not learned to walk in faith.

Joshua and Caleb were two of twelve leaders chosen to represent their tribes in spying out the Land of Promise. All twelve spies saw the same land and the same people. But ten saw it through natural eyes of fear, while two, Joshua and Caleb, saw the opportunity through the eyes of faith.

Then they told him, and said: "We went to the land where you sent us. It truly flows with milk and honey, and this is its fruit. Nevertheless the people who dwell in the land are strong; the cities are fortified and very large; moreover we saw the descendants of Anak there. . .

*"We are not able to go up against the people, for they are stronger than us. And they gave the children of Israel **a bad report** of the land which they had spied out, saying, "The land through which we have gone as spies is a land that devours its inhabitants, and all the people whom we saw in it are men of great stature. There we saw the giants (the descendants of Anak came from the giants); and we were like grasshoppers in our own sight, and so we were in their sight."* (Numbers 13:27–28, 31–33, emphasis mine)

So what did Joshua and Caleb do in the face of this unbelief? They stated their belief that God was in their midst, that He would be their Mighty Warrior, and that they must act in faith immediately.

Then Caleb quieted the people before Moses, and said, "Let us go up at once and take possession, for we are well able to overcome it." (Numbers 13:30)

They stated their belief that God was in their midst, that He would be their Mighty Warrior, and that they must act in faith immediately.

What was the difference between the two reports? Ten of the men focused on the giants and became afraid. Two of them focused on God and His promises and became inspired. They looked beyond the giants and all the mighty armies of the seven nations of Canaan to the promises of God.

Joshua had a foundation for his great faith. He remembered the promise that God made to his father Abraham. Abraham walked in the very land that Joshua walked in as a spy. And perhaps Joshua remembered the promise God gave to Abraham.

Then the LORD appeared to Abram and said, "To your descendants I will give this land." And there he built an altar to the LORD, who had appeared to him. (Genesis 12:7)

Then He said to Abram: "Know certainly that your descendants will be strangers in a land that is not theirs, and will serve them, and they will afflict them four hundred years. And also the nation whom they serve I will judge; afterward they shall come out with great possessions" (Genesis 15:13–14)

To your descendants I have given this land, from the river of Egypt to the great river, the River Euphrates." (Genesis 15:18)

Joshua also heard Moses declare God's promises. Moses learned about the character of God at the Burning Bush. As he spent forty years on the backside of the desert, Moses learned that God had not forgotten him. He remembered God's sure promises and passed that confidence to Joshua. And Joshua was among those that believed God.

> *Moses learned that God had not forgotten him. He remembered God's sure promises and passed that confidence to Joshua.*

> *So I have come down to deliver them out of the hand of the Egyptians, and to bring them up from that land to a good and large land, to a land flowing with milk and honey, to the place of the Canaanites and the Hittites and the Amorites and the Perizzites and the Hivites and the Jebusites.* (Exodus 3:8)

> *So the people **believed**; and when they heard that the LORD had visited the children of Israel and that He had looked on their affliction, then they bowed their heads and worshiped.* (Exodus 4:31, emphasis mine)

Joshua's faith in God was confirmed over and over as God's power was displayed through the ten plagues, the victory at the Rea Sea, God's continual provision of manna and water in the wilderness, and God's presence in the glory cloud. His faith was progressively growing stronger. Joshua's faith did not waver in the face of the giants and the great armies of the nations of Canaan.

It would have been easy for Joshua to see the fortified city of Jericho and waver. But he did not. He remained confident that despite the circumstances, God was able to win the battle. When he saw the giants in the land, his faith did not falter. When he saw the armies equipped with the most modern weapons and horses and chariots of iron, his faith stayed strong.

How do you see yourself? Are you strong and independent? That's a setup for failure. Are you a "nobody" that will never make a difference? Or are you God's servant, called and empowered by Him to do what He has called you to do?

Joshua could have seen himself as merely as a servant sent to spy out the land and bring back a report. But instead he saw himself as God's man for the moment.

The Bible tells us that God's eyes run back and forth throughout the whole earth to find a person whose heart is loyal to him (2 Chronicles 16:9). God had found his soldier who would lead Israel in the conquest of Canaan. At this point, Joshua was not aware that God would later choose him to become Moses' successor. He was simply being obedient in the moment. And that's exactly what God calls you and me to do.

E. As a servant, Joshua learned the principle of consecration.

Consecration carries the idea of being set apart to God. God calls us, and we surrender fully to His will. Consecration is not half-hearted business. We put our yes on the table and then let Him call the shots.

God had a purpose for Joshua. And Joshua would be faithful to God first as a servant and follower of Moses and then as God's soldier and leader of Israel. God saw his faithfulness and acknowledged it:

> *Except Caleb the son of Jephunneh, the Kenizzite, and Joshua the son of Nun, **for they have wholly followed the LORD.*** (Numbers 32:12, emphasis mine)

The phrase *wholly followed* carries the idea of a ship pulling up its anchor and fully opening its sails to catch the full power of the wind to move the ship. God's power is wholly available to those who trust Him fully and abandon all to Him.

Before Moses' death, he pleaded with God to place a shepherd-leader over Israel so that the congregation would not be like sheep without a shepherd. Moses trusted that God knew the hearts of all men and had been preparing the man for the mission. The one God chose to consecrate before all Israel in a formal and public ceremony had already been fully consecrated to God as Moses' servant. That man was Joshua.

> *Then Moses spoke to the LORD, saying: "Let the LORD, the God of the spirits of all flesh, set a man over the congregation, who may go out before them and go in before them, who may lead them out and bring them in, that the congregation of the LORD may not be like sheep which have no shepherd."*
>
> *And the LORD said to Moses: "Take Joshua the son of Nun with you, a man in whom is the Spirit, and lay your hand on him; set him before Eleazar the priest and before all the congregation, and inaugurate him in their sight. And you shall give some of your authority to him, that all the congregation of the children of Israel may be obedient. He shall stand before Eleazar the priest, who shall inquire before the LORD for him by the judgment of the Urim. At his word they shall go out, and at his word they shall come in, he and all the children of Israel with him—all the congregation."*
>
> *So Moses did as the LORD commanded him. He took Joshua and set him before Eleazar the priest and before all the congregation. And he laid his hands on him and*

inaugurated him, just as the LORD commanded by the hand of Moses.
(Numbers 27:15–23)

Joshua the servant would become the shepherd-leader of Israel. His main assignment would be to lead as God's soldier in the conquest of Canaan through war and then the dividing the land as the inheritance to the twelve tribes of Israel.

A soldier is expected to be fully consecrated to his commander in chief. He has one job—to obey and please his commander. He cannot allow himself to get entangled with lesser things, for he has a higher calling.

> *You therefore must endure hardship as a good soldier of Jesus Christ. No one engaged in warfare entangles himself with the affairs of this life, that he may please him who enlisted him as a soldier.* (2 Timothy 2:3–4)

A soldier is expected to be fully consecrated to his commander in chief. He has one job —to obey and please his commander. He cannot allow himself to get entangled with lesser things for he has a higher calling.

Jesus made it clear that His faithful followers could not serve two masters.

> *No one can serve two masters; for either he will hate the one and love the other, or else he will be loyal to the one and despise the other. You cannot serve God and mammon.* (Matthew 6:24)

Joshua was chosen to be God's soldier leader of Israel because he had personal consecration as a servant. God Himself professed that Joshua *wholly followed the Lord.*

Joshua could not have been an effective soldier had he not fully followed the Lord. Many times, we settle for partial obedience to Jesus. We obey the parts of the Bible we want to follow and disregard the rest.

Many times, we settle for partial obedience to Jesus.
We obey the parts of the Bible we want to follow and disregard the rest.

We cannot be effective in spiritual warfare if we are half-hearted Christians. We have no power against spiritual principalities and powers unless we are soldiers under the authority and obedience of our commander in chief, the Lord Jesus.

Demons mock weekend warriors who play church for an hour and do not endure hardness as good soldiers of Jesus Christ. Soldiers who do not reflect the character and moral purity of their Lord cannot pull down strongholds, bind the powers of darkness, or lead one of Satan's slaves to salvation in Jesus Christ.

The soldier must be consecrated fully to Jesus Christ. Consecration is a matter of the will. We must choose to fully follow the Lord (Ephesians 4:22–24).

> *The soldier must be consecrated fully to Jesus Christ. Consecration is a matter of the will. We must choose to fully follow the Lord.*

A Few Concluding Principles

Have you ever thought about the fact that **both** reports given back to Moses were accurate? The ten saw what they wanted to see—giants who could not possibly be defeated! Joshua and Caleb saw what God wanted them to see. They also reported truthfully: *God's hand was in this and they needed to seize the moment.* As we close this study from Numbers 13:27–33, we can see the following:

- ☐ Faith sees beyond the problem to the promises of God.

- ☐ Faith is centered in the will of God and not in our emotions.

- ☐ Faith depends on God's power and not in our own power.

- ☐ Faith will ensure victory but doubt will ensure defeat.

Take a moment and reflect on those four statements. In what ways do they speak to you and your circumstances right now?

"Faith" Statement	What does it mean to me right now?
Faith sees beyond the problem to the promises of God.	
Faith is centered in the will and not in our emotions.	
Faith depends on God's power and not in our own power.	
Faith will ensure victory but doubt will ensure defeat.	

The last three chapters have focused on two words: ***intercession*** and ***dependence.*** We pray in faith and according to His promises. We obey in total dependence.

No soldier is ready to drive out the enemy from his possession who has not been faithful as a servant. The choice is yours. What are you going to do?

 **Application**

Joshua had learned the principle of submission as he served Moses.

Cork and his wife Sue had come to Christ in our ministry. Not long after his conversion, Cork said to me, "I want to make your ministry successful. Anything you want me to do at church I will try to do." As a young pastor, I had never had a church member verbalize such a servant's heart.

It wasn't long after that, Cork felt called to be a pastor. Our church helped him launch a new church plant. He was a faithful pastor to that church for over thirty-five years and until the Lord called him home to heaven.

Perhaps you could follow the example of Cork and Sue and say to your pastor, "I want to help your ministry at church prosper. How can I serve you?"

Write below a statement in this section that spoke to you.

06   The Deadliest Battle: The Battle Within

Putting Things in Perspective

Joshua's first battle occurred at the Red Sea. It pictures the soldier of Christ standing still and waiting for the deliverance of God. It becomes a perfect representation of our salvation: God does it all. We bring nothing but our sin. He gives us all His blessings. Ephesians 1:3 tells us that God has blessed us with *every spiritual blessing in the heavenly places in Christ.* We didn't contribute anything to that transaction. It was all by grace through faith.

Joshua's second battle was against Amalek. While Joshua and his troops fought the physical battle in the valley, Moses fought the spiritual battle on the mountain top. Joshua fought as God told him to, in dependence on the Spirit of God and according to the truth of the Word of God. Moses prayed as God told him to, with faith, aided by his companions Aaron and Hur. This dual picture of intercession and dependence is a perfect representation of the process of sanctification in our Christian life. God empowers; we obey.

These two battles are foundational for every other battle Israel will face in their history. Knowing that *Salvation belongs to the Lord* (the lesson from the first battle) and that *Intercession and Dependence* are critical to our success (the lesson from the second battle), we now we come to the third battle—and it is entirely different from the other two. It doesn't occur on a battlefield. In fact, you can't even see it if you are looking at things from a human perspective. It's the battle *within.* And it's perhaps the deadliest of all the battles. It is pictured in Exodus 32.

☐   In the first battle, the Lord fought **for** Israel.

☐   In the second battle, the Lord fought **with** Israel.

☐   In this third battle, the Lord fought **against** Israel.

The Red Sea: Salvation by Grace | Amalek: Intercession and Dependence | The Battle Within: Putting to Death Our Old Desires

69

A Current Battle

Three US soldiers had been killed and another wounded during a joint US-Afghan military operation in Nangarhar province, US officials told CNN. An American official said the soldiers were shot in an apparent *insider attack,* also known as a "green-on-blue" incident because of the color-coding system used by NATO. During such assaults, members of the Afghan security forces are known to target US and other NATO soldiers.

> *"A Mujahid (freedom fighter) infiltrator of the Islamic Emirate who had enrolled himself in the Kabul government's army attacked American soldiers."* [12]

It was an inside job.

One of the most difficult strategies of the enemy to detect is when he turns soldiers against their own troops. The insurgents wait for an opportune time to launch a secret attack. Soldiers who become turncoats and sabotage their own army are deadly.

Israel had seen God fight for them at the Red Sea and defeat Pharaoh and his army. Then Israel saw God fight with them as they battled Amalek with the sword as Moses interceded for them. Now Israel faces a third battle—one caused by their idolatry and their rejection of God for a golden calf.

What defeated Israel at this point was their inner, sinful desires. It was also an inside job.

What "inside jobs" are getting to you right now?

My "Inside Battles"	How They Are Affecting Me?	What Do I Need to Do?

---

[12] By Ryan Browne, Barbara Starr and Ray Sanchez, CNN. Updated 10:20 PM ET, Mon June 12, 2017.

The Battle Begins

Moses was called up to Mount Sinai to meet with God personally. It was the ultimate come-to-Jesus meeting. There God spoke to Moses, giving him instructions, laws, and principles that would keep Israel on track, faithful to their God. Exodus 31 ends with a simple statement: *When He had finished speaking with him upon Mount Sinai, He gave Moses the two tablets of the testimony, tablets of stone, written by the finger of God.*

There it was. The Decalogue. The Ten Commandments, written by the finger of God. It's one thing for us to hold our Bibles in our hands and say, "This is God's Word." And it is. It is wholly true and inspired—without error. It is the very Word of God. But it was also typeset by professionals. It was printed, bound, and packaged at a publishing house. And sometimes we take it for granted. But in Moses' case, this revelation was different. God literally stenciled the Hebrew letters onto the tablets of stone that Moses was carrying.

Who could deny that Moses met personally with God? Who could argue with what God wrote on those tablets? But Israel ignored it. They rebelled against it. As Exodus 32:8 says, they *quickly turned aside* from God's ways. What did they do?

- ☐ They made a molten calf.
- ☐ They worshiped it.
- ☐ They sacrificed to it.
- ☐ They ascribed miraculous powers to it, saying that *this idol* delivered them from the land of Egypt.

Israel hadn't seen God do very much in their lives recently. (*Dear reader, you should sense the sarcasm dripping through.*) They had only seen Him:

- ☐ Send ten plagues upon their Egyptian enemies.
- ☐ Part the Red Sea and deliver them from Pharaoh's hand.
- ☐ Lead them with a pillar and cloud of fire daily.
- ☐ Miraculously provide food and water to meet their needs of hunger and thirst daily.
- ☐ Fight for them and with them against Amalek.
- ☐ Give them refreshment, provide godly leadership for them, and care for them as a loving, heavenly Father.

But when Moses is gone for days at Mount Sinai, they decide to take matters into their own hands. They conclude they need a god they can see, and touch, and shape into whatever they want it to be. Bottom line? They want to be in control.

Israel decided to take matters into their own hands. They concluded they need a god they could see, and touch, and shape into whatever they want it to be. Bottom line? They wanted to be in control.

Does that remind you of anyone? Perhaps someone you saw in the mirror this morning?

Here's a word that is hard for all of us: **submission.** We don't like that word. And we certainly don't like the concept. But that's what God calls us to do. The word is *hupotasso,* a Greek military term meaning "to arrange – in troop divisions; to put in subjection." It is used thirty-one times in the New Testament. Six of those times are in the small letter of 1 Peter.

- ☐ 2:13 *Submit yourselves for the Lord's sake to every human institution, whether to a king as the one in authority.*
- ☐ 2:18 *Servants, be submissive to your masters with all respect, not only to those who are good and gentle, but also to those who are unreasonable.*
- ☐ 3:1 *In the same way, you wives, be submissive to your own husbands so that even if any of them are disobedient to the word, they may be won without a word by the behavior of their wives.*
- ☐ 3:5 *For in this way in former times the holy women also, who hoped in God, used to adorn themselves, being submissive to their own husbands.*
- ☐ 3:22 *(Jesus Christ), who is at the right hand of God, having gone into heaven, after angels and authorities and powers had been subjected to Him.*
- ☐ 5:5 *You younger men, likewise, be subject to your elders; and all of you, clothe yourselves with humility toward one another, for "God resists the proud, but gives grace to the humble."*

That's a lot of repetition. All of us must submit to government authorities; workers must submit to their bosses; wives to their husbands; angels were subject to Jesus; and younger men to their elders; and all of us must be subject toward each other.

Why? Peter is making a point. He wants us to experience the fullness of God's grace. And that grace is given to the humble—those who willingly submit to God and to each other.

> *God wants us to experience the fulness of His grace. And that grace is given to the humble—those who willingly submit to God and to each other.*

You may be thinking, *They had seen God do **everything** for them, and yet they still rebelled.* Yes … just like you and me.

Sometimes we forget what God has done for us. Sometimes we become overwhelmed by our emotions. Other times, circumstances get to us so badly that we become fearful and afraid, and we withdraw … from God, from the disciplines of grace, and from the support of others.

What do we need to do? First, we need to **remember.** Second, we need to **stay in the battle and refuse to withdraw**. Living by faith sometimes means that we just choose *not to give up, not to withdraw, not to isolate ourselves from the body of Christ.* We need to **submit.**

Israel never did that. They never bowed the knee. They never submitted. Their posture was one of "waiting to rebel." Outwardly, they still looked good—but inside, they had already taken steps away from God. They were simply biding their time. And they got their chance when Moses left for the mountain.

What Happened Next?

Good things happen when we are alone with God. And at times, some bad things also happen. As Moses was alone with God on Mt. Sinai, Joshua was also alone, waiting patiently for him to return. In the events that followed, Joshua learned the high value God placed on His holiness. God made this clear to Joshua as he observed Moses. If God's presence and power was to go with Israel, then His people must judge both their personal sins and open sins in the camp of Israel.

> *Good things happen when we are alone with God.*
> *And at times, some bad things also happen.*

But the people were impatient. They could not wait on Moses or trust God when Moses was absent. Their fleshly sin nature was aroused by a vocal group of rebels who demanded Aaron make gods for them to follow.

> *Now when the people saw that Moses delayed coming down from the mountain, the people gathered together to Aaron, and said to him, "Come, make us gods that shall go before us; for as for this Moses, the man who brought us up out of the land of Egypt, we do not know what has become of him."* (Exodus 32:1)

What a contrast! Moses stood with God. Aaron stood on the side of the people, against God. He instructed the people to give him their golden earrings. He fashioned a golden calf like the idols they had seen in Egypt. What followed proved that many who had been delivered out of Egypt still had "Egypt" in them. Aaron called for a feast to the Lord, but it was a lustful worship of demon gods of Egypt. Aaron could not, or would not, restrain the people in their open idolatry (Exodus 32:1–6, 25).

> *Now when Moses saw that the people were unrestrained (for Aaron had not restrained them, to their shame among their enemies.)* (Exodus 32:25)

Though Moses interceded to God not to destroy the people for their great sin, He so identified with God's holiness that he was angry over their rebellion (Exodus 32:10–14). With holy zeal and righteous indignation against those who sinned openly and showed no remorse over their sin, he called for an elite group of soldiers to stand with him on the side of God's holiness:

> *"Whoever is on the LORD's side—come to me!" And all the sons of Levi gathered themselves together to him. And he said to them, "Thus says the LORD God of Israel: 'Let every man put*

his sword on his side, and go in and out from entrance to entrance throughout the camp, and let every man kill his brother, every man his companion, and every man his neighbor.'" (Exodus 32:26–27)

Moses called for a sword against those unrepentant idolaters in the camp. That day the sons of Levi killed three thousand. Unlike striking down their enemies like Amalek with the sword, they were striking down their brothers, friends, and neighbors. This was a great test of faith that set their loyalty to God at odds with their loyalty to their own countrymen. Out of God's holiness, the Lord fought against Israel that day.

This was a great test of faith that set their loyalty to God at odds with their loyalty to their own countrymen.

Lessons for Joshua ... and Us

What can we learn from this event?

☐ We must take God seriously.

God is holy. We must see Him for who He is: high and lifted up, majestic in glory, all-powerful, transcendent, and worthy of all our praise. Take some time to read through John's description of Jesus in Revelation 1:9–16. It will fill you with praise for our great God, but it will also remind you of your smallness. John *fell at His feet like a dead man.* He was consumed with the total awesomeness of Jesus Christ.

Are you consumed with the total awesomeness of Jesus?

☐ Our worship of Him must be grounded in personal holiness.

We are His children, sons and daughters of the King. But we must also realize we are sinners who must humbly appropriate the means of grace for personal forgiveness and cleansing. Worship always starts with personal cleansing.

One of the prevalent sins in our Christian culture is taking God too lightly. God is a God of love, grace, forgiveness, and tenderness. But He is also a God of holiness, power, might, majesty, and glory.

Don't give the devil an opportunity, Paul says in Ephesians 4:27. Some translations render that word *"a foothold."* It is literally "a place, a beach-head, from which he can gain control and influence." Sinful attitudes and actions often start small. But they are fueled from the fire of rebellion and lack of submission.

What do we need to do? We must fight for holiness. We must battle for personal purity. And we must not give the Devil *a place.*

Fight for holiness. Battle for purity. Don't give the Devil a place.

☐ Leaders must be like Moses, standing with God against sin, but pleading with God for sinners.

Moses prayed that God would graciously spare His people (Exodus 32:11–14). As intercessors, we represent our people to God. As preachers, we represent our God to our people. Stand with God. Speak truth to people. Be gracious toward them and pray for them sincerely.

☐ Leaders must not be like Aaron, who compromised God's holiness and was manipulated by the rebellious.

God did not allow His presence to go before the people to the Promised Land without repentance (Exodus 33:3). If you want the blessings of God on your life, you must refuse to compromise.

If you want the blessings of God on your life, you must refuse to compromise.

☐ We must remember that we do not fight with swords or physical weapons. We fight a spiritual warfare.

> For **the weapons of our warfare** are not carnal but mighty in God for pulling down strongholds. (2 Corinthians 10:4, emphasis mine)

The soldier soon learns that he must fight this spiritual war on three fronts: against the world, the flesh, and the Devil. They are all enemies of our soul and mission with Christ.

Of all our enemies, the greatest lies within us, in our own flesh.

> But I see another law in my members, **warring against the law of my mind,** and bringing me into captivity to the law of sin which is in my members. O wretched man that I am! Who will deliver me from this body of death? I thank God—through Jesus Christ our Lord! (Romans 7:23–24, emphasis mine)

> Beloved, I beg you as sojourners and pilgrims, abstain from fleshly lusts which **war against the soul.** (1 Peter 2:11, emphasis mine)

A good soldier is trained to know the strengths and weaknesses of his enemy. One good spiritual exercise that helps train a spiritual soldier for warfare is to learn from all the good and bad experiences written about every Bible character. When you look at characters in the Bible, there are two questions you should always ask:

1. What do I see in them that is the work of God's grace that I should seek?
2. What do I see in them that is a manifestation of the sinful nature of the flesh?

Every time we see people in the Bible fall into sin, we should say "There go I, except for the grace of God." We are never so strong that we cannot sin. We are never so strong that we don't need to be totally dependent on Jesus.

We are never so strong that we cannot sin.
We are never so strong that we don't need to be totally dependent on Jesus.

There was a time when the apostle Paul thought that he kept the law blamelessly and was righteous by his own merit. However, when he saw Christ and His righteousness, then all of Paul's self-righteousness became recognized for what it really was: filthy, sinful pride (Philippians 3:4–10).

Paul recognized the nature of his old self-life: *For I know that in me (that is, in my flesh) nothing good dwells* (Romans 7:18).

Let's apply this principle to some of the Bible characters in our context of Exodus 32.

In Moses, we can see God's deep work of grace in his life. He knew God. He knew God's grace. And like Moses, we need to learn to wait before God. We need to identify with God's holiness and hate sin. We need to act as intercessors and plead with God for people. And we need to call God's people to take a stand with God and against sin. It is important to remember that those in leadership may sometimes have to exercise spiritual discipline against the unrepentant.

In Aaron, we can see the weakness of the flesh evidenced in his life. He compromised under pressure from the people. Just like we learned some positive lessons from the life of Moses, we must also learn some *negative* ones from Aaron. We must not fear people who pressure us to compromise truth. We must be willing to stand with truth, even if we are to suffer for it. Remember, yesterday's blessings are no guarantee of today's spiritual success. Those who experienced God's grace yesterday can still manifest the worst of the flesh under pressure today. The flesh can still blame others when it is reproved for sin. Aaron said that the people were "set on evil" (Exodus 32:22). Aaron's reaction was just like Adam and

76

Eve's. Adam basically said, "It is the fault of the woman you gave me. And God, it's ultimately Your fault because You gave her to me." Eve said, "It is the fault of the serpent."

We can also learn lessons from the nation of Israel. **In Israel**, we see our flesh in action. But we must learn that our flesh is impatient. It cannot wait on God. Our flesh will oppose the authority of God and those who are set over us. Our flesh can tell God today, *"All that you command we will do,"* and then turn around tomorrow to worship the works of our own hands. And finally, our flesh can delight in worship that is man-centered and stirs up the emotions and passions of the flesh and be devoid of the holiness of God.

> *Our flesh can delight in worship that is man-centered and stirs up the emotions and passions of the flesh and be devoid of the holiness of God.*

The Bible tells us that we will battle with our flesh the rest of our lives.

> *Therefore, put to death your members which are on the earth: fornication, uncleanness, passion, evil desire, and covetousness, which is idolatry. Because of these things the wrath of God is coming upon the sons of disobedience, in which you yourselves once walked when you lived in them.* (Colossians 3:5–7)

> *Now the works of the flesh are evident, which are: adultery, fornication, uncleanness, lewdness, idolatry, sorcery, hatred, contentions, jealousies, outbursts of wrath, selfish ambitions, dissensions, heresies, envy, murders, drunkenness, revelries, and the like; of which I tell you beforehand, just as I also told you in time past, that those who practice such things will not inherit the kingdom of God.* (Galatians 5:19–21)

We are not fit for battle if we do not daily die to self and put to death the flesh. Ultimately it all gets back to that whole concept of submission.

> *And those who are Christ's have crucified the flesh with its passions and desires.* (Galatians 5:24)

> *Ultimately it all gets back to that whole concept of submission.*

From God's perspective, we have already been crucified with Christ through His death and resurrection.

> *I have been crucified with Christ; it is no longer I who live, but Christ lives in me; and the life which I now live in the flesh I live by faith in the Son of God, who loved me and gave Himself for me.* (Galatians 2:20)

We are to appropriate this knowledge and apply it to our life daily.

> *Knowing this, that our old man was crucified with Him, that the body of sin might be done away with, that we should no longer be slaves of sin. For he who has died has been freed from sin.* (Romans 6:6–7)

God is asking each of us, "Whose side are you on?" (Exodus 32:26). If we are truly on God's side, then we will come to Him ready to deal with the sinfulness of our flesh. We take God's side against our own self-life/flesh. We will refuse to tolerate even the little sins that can create the slippery slope, leading to greater sins.

The Power of a Changed Life

H. A. Ironside, a former pastor of Moody Church, began preaching one night in the open air of Chicago, attracting a large, enthusiastic gathering. During his message a man stepped out from the crowd and handed him a note. This particular man was a well-known agnostic, sowing skepticism and discord wherever the truth of Scripture was spoken, especially in relation to God being a personal God who seeks relationships with humans.

That is why, with face full of pride and self-confidence, he approached Ironside with a letter. The pastor opened the note and read the words aloud: "I challenge you to a debate in the Hall of Science next Sunday afternoon." Then he turned to the agnostic and delivered this wise response:

> *I will come and debate with you the reality of the Christian life, if you will do one thing; you must agree to bring with you one person from your sphere of influence. One person who was discouraged and defeated by life, not knowing where to turn or what to believe, until that person came and heard you lecture your agnostic beliefs. And then that man, after listening to you, said in effect, 'I believe what you are saying and will begin living in light of it.' Bring one person who, after hearing you speak, found peace of mind, victory over temptation, and a purpose for living. Bring one and I will debate you; and will bring with me one hundred.*

Upon hearing this, it was reported that the agnostic refused the offer and quickly turned away.

What a great reminder to us that the unanswerable argument for Christianity is, in fact, the Christian! It starts within us. Whom do people see when they see you? Do they sense that something is different about you? Do they see the hand of God on your life? Or have you compromised and conformed to the ways of the world.

Your choice. But I implore you: walk with Him today!

 **Application**

Israel had rebels against God's holiness within the camp. Have you recognized that we too have a rebel within our own flesh? Have you purposed to stand with the Lord in this battle against your own self-life? Write out a prayer that expresses this.

Defining Moments

In this chapter, we are going to see one of Israel's defining moments. It forever changed the lives of those on the journey from Egypt to the Promised Land. In fact, as a result of their choices, they never got there. They died in the wilderness, never experiencing the blessings of the Promise. And it all started with … unbelief.

Unbelief … did you know that Jesus rebuked the disciples for their unbelief? We might give them the name, "O men of little faith." We'll call them *OMOLFs,* for short. But it wasn't just first-century disciples that were *OMOLFs.* Those of us who claim to follow Jesus today are all too often *men and women of little faith.* And so were the men and women of Israel who were following Moses in the wilderness.

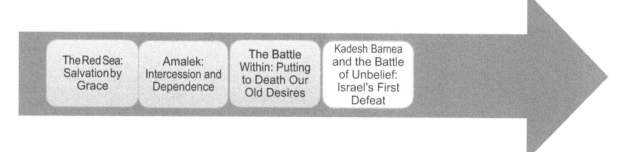

The Road Toward Unbelief

Joshua saw Israel's great victory at the Red Sea. He was then chosen to lead Israel against Amalek when they first attacked Israel (Exodus 17:8–16). With Moses' prayers and God's power, they won. Later, he was chosen as one of twelve spies to bring back a report of the Promised Land. Joshua's faith in God helped him see that victory was possible (Numbers 13).

But after Moses, Joshua, and Caleb pleaded with Israel to march forward to victory, Israel rebelled because of fear and unbelief (Numbers 14). At this point, God determined they would spend the rest of their lives wandering in the wilderness. That generation would never see the good land God had promised. God killed the ten spies who brought the evil report to the leaders. But Joshua and Caleb were spared, and both were promised that they would indeed inherit the land they had walked upon. (Sometimes longevity is not determined by our genes but by our faith in God's promise and purpose.)

In a show of false repentance, Israel cried out to God, *"We have sinned"* and armed themselves to go forward into battle. However, they had already been defeated by unbelief.

Then Moses told these words to all the children of Israel, and the people mourned greatly. And they rose early in the morning and went up to the top of the mountain, saying, "Here we are, and we will go up to the place which the LORD has promised, for we have sinned!"

And Moses said, "Now why do you transgress the command of the LORD? For this will not succeed. Do not go up, lest you be defeated by your enemies, for the LORD is not among you. For the Amalekites and the Canaanites are there before you, and you shall fall by the sword; because you have turned away from the LORD, the LORD will not be with you."

But they presumed to go up to the mountaintop. Nevertheless, neither the ark of the covenant of the LORD nor Moses departed from the camp. Then the Amalekites and the Canaanites who dwelt in that mountain came down and attacked them, and drove them back as far as Hormah. (Numbers 14:39–45)

They had already been defeated by unbelief before they went to war.

Joshua saw with his own eyes the great cost of unbelief. No doubt many of the soldiers that went to war with the Amalekites and Canaanites had a sense of self-confidence because they had previously participated in Amalek's defeat. But what they failed to understand was that their victory was not accomplished by their own strength. It was because of their faith-commitment to the Lord.

- [ ] In the first battle, the Lord fought **for** Israel.

- [ ] In the second battle, the Lord fought **with** Israel.

- [ ] In this third battle, the Lord fought **against** Israel.

- [ ] In the fourth battle, the Lord **was not with** Israel.

Contrasting Battles

Israel battles Amalek twice. But they are very different battles with very different results.

In the first battle with Amalek (Exodus 17):

- [ ] God told them to go and fight (v. 9).
- [ ] They believed God and went in faith.
- [ ] They had God-appointed leaders in Moses and Joshua to follow (v. 10).
- [ ] They had the Lord to fight with them.
- [ ] They had the Rod of God lifted high as a symbol of dependence upon God (v. 9).
- [ ] They defeated Amalek.

Notice the differences in the second battle with Amalek (Numbers 14):

- ☐ God told them not to go to battle (v. 42).
- ☐ They did not go in faith but went into battle presumptuously, in their own strength (v. 44).
- ☐ They were told that they would be defeated, yet they blindly went ahead (v. 41).
- ☐ None of their leaders went with them (v. 44).
- ☐ The Lord did not go with them nor did the Ark of the Covenant (vv. 43–44).
- ☐ They did not have the flag of God, "The Lord is my banner," to march under (v. 43).
- ☐ They were defeated by Amalek (v. 45)

Why Israel Lost

This battle was first lost in their hearts before it was lost on the battlefield. Unbelief is a contagious disease that the ten spies caught while viewing the Promised Land. It turned their faith into fear. They refused to believe the promises of God. Ten men, each handpicked leaders of their tribes, allowed their flesh and Satan's whispers of doubt to turn them into cowards and failures. Then their words of unbelief were like a fire spreading destruction throughout the camp of Israel.

Then they told him, and said: "We went to the land where you sent us. It truly flows with milk and honey, and this is its fruit. Nevertheless, the people who dwell in the land are strong; the cities are fortified and very large; moreover, we saw the descendants of Anak there. (Numbers 13:27–28)

This battle was first lost in the heart before it was lost on the battlefield.

Nevertheless, this was a turning point for them.

- ☐ God promised the good land to Abraham.
- ☐ God sent Moses to deliver them and lead them into the Promised Land.
- ☐ God demonstrated His power with ten plagues on Egypt.
- ☐ God defeated Pharaoh's army at the Red Sea as Israel stood still and watched their great God.
- ☐ God already gave them a sample of victory over Amalek and the nations of Canaan as firstfruits of greater victories to come.

God gave them a foundation for faith, but they chose to believe their circumstances and walked by sight.

Notice the progression (or should I say *regression*) away from a walk of faith.

| God tells them to go spy out the land and come back with a report. | They see the giants and turn their eyes from God (faith) to their circumstances (fear). | They bring back a negative report ... causing the people to grumble and complain against God. |

| The nation responds in unbelief and rebels against God. | The men who brought up the bad report died by plague before the Lord. | The nation, acting independently from God, presumptuously goes into battle and is defeated. |

Why Is This Battle, and Its Backstory, So Important to Us?

The stories in the Old Testament are not given simply as a historical record. They are given as examples for us. Sometimes the example is a positive one that we should emulate. Other times, the example is a negative one, warning us of the dangers of failing to live by faith.

> *Now these things happened to them as **an example**, but they were written down **for our instruction**, on whom the end of the ages has come.* (1 Corinthians 10:11, emphasis mine)

We must look into the mirror of the Word and see our own reflection and be warned. We're capable of making the same wrong choices Israel did. We have the very Word of God to read with our own eyes and to believe and march forward into our inheritance in Christ. However, we often follow this same pattern of unbelief and do not become God's soldiers, advancing His kingdom.

God's Word marks this battle as an example, warning us when we come to the border of God's great calling for us. Victory is ours in Christ—if we walk in faith and obedience. But when we don't—when we choose to run in fear like Israel at Kadesh Barnea—we will suffer the consequences.

Victory is ours in Christ—if we walk in faith and obedience. But when we don't —when we choose to run in fear like Israel at Kadesh Barnea— we will suffer the consequences.

God would not have repeated this battle and its context so often in Scripture if it were not critical in the life of the soldier of Christ. If God emphasizes this event over and over in Scripture, it is because we must make a clear and correct choice in the day of battle. Our lives depend on it.

God considered the lessons learned from the unbelief of Israel so important that He gave us over two hundred verses related to this event. [13] Take the time to look up each of these passages.

Copy this chart into a notebook to record the insights you gain from God's Word.

Bible Passage	What do I learn from this? How does it affect my faith-choices?
(see footnote below)	

Now, take a few moments in prayerful reflection. Ask the Holy Spirit to speak to you. "Do I retreat in unbelief? Do I let the giants of my circumstances keep me from what the Father has promised?"

All of us must make critical choices about some step of faith God is calling us to make. Will we believe Him … or will we let the giants keep us from our inheritance?

Will we believe Him … or will we let the giants keep us from our inheritance?

Caleb and Joshua challenged the people to go in faith. But Israel walked in fear:

Then Caleb quieted the people before Moses, and said, "Let us go up at once and take possession, for we are well able to overcome it." But the men who had gone up with him said, "We are not able to go up against the people, for they are stronger than we." And they gave the children of Israel a bad report of the land which they had spied out, saying, "The land through which we have gone as spies is a land that devours its inhabitants, and all the people whom we saw in it are men of great stature. There we saw the giants (the descendants of Anak came from the giants); and we were like grasshoppers in our own sight, and so we were in their sight." (Numbers 13:30–33)

As the entire congregation wept and complained, *"If only we had died in the land of Egypt! Or if*

---

[13] Numbers 13, 14, 20, 26:64–65; 32:6-15; Deuteronomy 1:19–46, 2:13–25, 9:22–24; Joshua 14:6–15; Psalm 78:8–10; Psalm 95:7–11; Psalm 106:24–27; 1 Corinthians 10:1–13; Hebrews 3:16–19, 4:1–11; Jude 5.

only we had died in this wilderness!" (Numbers 14:1–2), Joshua and Caleb challenged them to believe God and to go up and take the land:

> *Only do not rebel against the LORD, nor fear the people of the land, for they are our bread; their protection has departed from them, and the LORD is with us. Do not fear them.* (Numbers 14:9)

Joshua reminded the people, *"The Lord is with us."*

- ☐ *Do not rebel against the Lord.*
- ☐ *Do not fear the people.*
- ☐ *They are bread for us.*
- ☐ *Their protection has departed.*
- ☐ *The Lord is with us.*
- ☐ *Do not fear them.*

The God Factor

Israel heard two reports concerning the Promised Land that day. There was a ***majority report*** that said, "We can't do it." It was motivated by fear—with eyes only on the circumstances. There was also a ***minority report.*** It was motivated by faith—with eyes on the promises of God.

Israel had a choice. They could believe the evil report of doubt from the ten spies or the good report of faith from Caleb and Joshua. They chose to believe the evil report that did not factor in God who had **fought for them** at the Red Sea and had **fought with them** against Amalek. Therefore, they would experience the Lord **who did not go with them** at Kadesh Barnea.

This event was a last straw with God and a turning point for those who refused to believe God. They would all die in the wilderness just as they had spoken.

> *Say to them, "As I live," says the LORD, "just as you have spoken in My hearing, so I will do to you: The carcasses of you who have complained against Me shall fall in this wilderness, all of you who were numbered, according to your entire number, from twenty years old and above. Except for Caleb the son of Jephunneh and Joshua the son of Nun, you shall by no means enter the land which I swore I would make you dwell in."* (Numbers 14:28–30)

All of us face a series of choices every day. Some are big—major life decisions. And they will be turning points in our lives, either for good or for evil. Some are small choices. But even though small, they will still be determinative. They are opportunities to choose to live by faith and grow strong in our God. How do we make the right choices? We see God in the midst of our choices. No matter how many are against you, God plus you equals a majority in every situation. The God-factor makes a difference.

Lessons for Us Today

What are the lessons for the soldiers of Christ today?

1. We must walk by faith and not by sight. There will be people who don't understand your faith in God. They cannot *"see"* it. Of course not! *Faith is the assurance of things hoped for, the conviction of things not seen* (Hebrews 11:1). Don't expect others to see what you see. Don't be swayed by the crowd. *See* what God chooses to reveal to you. And obey that.

2. We must bring every thought of doubt into submission to Christ. *For the weapons of our warfare are not carnal but mighty in God for pulling down strongholds, casting down arguments and every high thing that exalts itself against the knowledge of God, bringing every thought into captivity to the obedience of Christ, and being ready to punish all disobedience when your obedience is fulfilled.* (2 Corinthians 10:4–6)

3. Look to others who are strong in faith. We should believe those who God appointed as our leaders to be examples of faith for us. God always has a Moses, a Caleb, and a Joshua who we can follow.

4. As soldiers, we must not presume that because we saw victory yesterday that victory today and tomorrow is guaranteed. We must exercise our faith and dependence on God every day.

5. We feed on truth and grow spiritually by accepting the challenge of faith. When Joshua said, *"They are bread for us,"* he was speaking out of the strong faith God had built in him.

6. The words of our mouth can **discourage faith** … or they can **build faith**. Watch your words. They make a difference—for you and for others. David had to tell himself, *"Bless the Lord, O my soul* (Psalm 103:1). He needed to *hear* that encouragement. So do you. And so do others. Speak truth. Speak encouragement. Tell yourself, out loud, that you need to trust God. And let that encouragement spill over to others.

More Words about Words

This subject of our words is so important that I want us to focus on it as we close this chapter.

Words are powerful weapons in the mouth of the soldier of Christ. They are more powerful than the sword of the enemy. They can defeat us or deliver us. In his New Testament letter, James uses three analogies to tell us the power of our words (James 3:2–12).

- First, he compares them to a bit in a horse's mouth. That small bit is able to bring the mighty horse under control. It's that powerful. Our words can build up someone and positively change their lives forever. Or they can tear someone down and negatively affect them for the rest of their lives.

- Second, he tells us that our words are like the rudder of a ship. That rudder, though very small, is able to turn a mighty ship in any direction it wants. They set the direction of our lives. I know men and women who have been inspired toward excellence in their careers because of encouragement they received. I know others who have kept trusting God in incredibly hard circumstances because they were encouraged by fellow believers. Your words make a difference.

- Finally, he compares the tongue to a fire that is able to set an entire forest ablaze. Our words can be like refreshing water or bitter poison. Wars have been started over angry words. Marriages have been destroyed because people could not control their tongues.

James concludes, *But no man can tame the tongue. It is an unruly evil, full of deadly poison. With it we bless our God and Father, and with it we curse men, who have been made in the similitude of God* (James 3:8–9).

Looking back on this important battle, we see how Satan used the fear and unbelief of ten spies with the power of discouraging words. God's people were not able to tame their tongue, and its poison was used to kill an entire generation of Israel.

*For when they went up to the Valley of Eshcol and saw the land, they **discouraged** the heart of the children of Israel, so that they did not go into the land which the LORD had given them.* (Numbers 32:9, emphasis mine)

Where can we go up? Our brethren have discouraged our hearts, saying, "The people are greater and taller than we; the cities are great and fortified up to heaven; moreover we have seen the sons of the Anakim there."

Then I said to you, "Do not be terrified, or afraid of them. The LORD your God, who goes before you, He will fight for you, according to all He did for you in Egypt before your eyes." (Deuteronomy 1:28–30)

It is sad to see this battle repeated in our churches today. It seems it is easier for the majority of the church to listen to those who are overcome by fear than it is to follow those who have conquered their fear with faith. This is why some churches do not grow and eventually decline and wander in the wilderness never reaching their potential. Listen to those who are like Moses, Joshua, and Caleb who challenge us to grow in Christ! Follow their lead!

Listen to those who are like Moses, Joshua, and Caleb who challenge us to grow in Christ! Follow their lead!

Finally, we should consider some of the words that were related to the context of this battle of unbelief at Kadesh Barnea. Take your Bible and look up each of these phrases. Underline or highlight them in your Bible so they will stand out to you whenever you read these passages.

- ☐ *Nevertheless, the people are strong.* Numbers 13:28
- ☐ *They are stronger than we.* Numbers 13:31
- ☐ *They gave a bad report.* Numbers 13:32
- ☐ *We were like grasshoppers in our own sight.* Numbers 13:33
- ☐ *The people wept and complained.* Numbers 14:1–2
- ☐ *If only we had died in the wilderness.* Numbers 14:2
- ☐ *Better to return to Egypt.* Numbers 14:3
- ☐ *Do not rebel against the Lord.* Numbers 14:9
- ☐ *Do not fear the people.* Numbers 14:9
- ☐ *Let us stone Joshua and Caleb.* Numbers 14:30
- ☐ *These people reject Me.* Numbers 14:11
- ☐ *These people do not believe Me.* Numbers 14:11
- ☐ *They will not see the Promised Land.* Numbers 14:23
- ☐ *You have turned away from the Lord and He will not be with you in battle.* Numbers 14:43
- ☐ *They presumed to go up to battle.* Numbers 14:44
- ☐ *They were driven back.* Numbers 14:45
- ☐ *They discouraged the heart of Israel.* Numbers 32:9
- ☐ *Because they have not wholly followed Me.* Numbers 32:11
- ☐ *God made them wander in the wilderness forty years until that generation that refused to believe Him had died.* Numbers 32:13
- ☐ *Nevertheless, you would not go up.* Deuteronomy 1:36
- ☐ *You complained and said the Lord hates us.* Deuteronomy 1:27

- *Our brothers have discouraged our hearts.* Deuteronomy 1:28
- *Do not be afraid – the Lord goes before you.* Deuteronomy 1:29–30
- *You did not believe the Lord.* Deuteronomy 1:32
- *You rebelled against God, did not believe or obey Him.* Deuteronomy 9:23
- *The evil spies made the heart of the people melt.* Joshua 14:8
- *Not faithful to God being armed turned back in the day of battle.* Psalm 78:8–9
- *They despised the pleasant land.* Psalm 106:24
- *Do not harden your hearts as in the rebellion.* Psalm 95:8
- *They rebelled.* Hebrews 3:16
- *They could not enter in because of unbelief.* Hebrews 3:19
- *Let us be diligent to enter into rest and not follow the same example of disobedience.* Hebrews 4:11

That generation left a damning legacy. Forever they will be known by those phrases in God's Word. And the warning of their lives and choices is directed toward us: we must not draw back in fear but be diligent to enter by faith the rest that God has promised us.

We must not draw back in fear
but be diligent to enter by faith the rest that God has promised us.

This battle is one of the most important battles in all of Scripture—not because of Israel's victory but because of their defeat. It showed Joshua the weakness of the flesh and the easiness by which we may be deceived. Satan defeats us more easily by words than by weapons.

In Hebrews 3, God warns us not to draw back through unbelief, but to go on into maturity and fruitfulness that is our promised inheritance in Christ. Notice the strong warning of words the author uses: *Beware, unbelief, departing, hardened,* and *deceitfulness.*

> **Beware**, brethren, lest there be in any of you an evil heart of **unbelief** in **departing** from the living God; but exhort one another daily, while it is called "Today," lest any of you be **hardened** through the **deceitfulness** of sin. For we have become partakers of Christ if we hold the beginning of our confidence steadfast to the end. (Hebrews 3:12–14, emphasis mine).

God also reminds us that we must have a positive faith that boldly claims our inheritance rest like Caleb with words like *hold the beginning of our confidence steadfast to the end.*

The negative example of that generation failing to enter the Promised Land of their inheritance through unbelief is used as a warning to us to be diligent. *Let us therefore be diligent to enter that rest, lest anyone fall according to the same example of disobedience* (Hebrews 4:11).

Fight the battle against unbelief. Win it with faith.

 **Application**

Considering that words have the power to build faith or discourage faith. What commitment will you make regarding your words?

When Battles Are Unprovoked

Tonya Harding. Does that name ring a bell? If you think back to the 1994 Olympics, you will remember her name. She was US champion in women's figure skating. But that wasn't enough. She wanted Olympic gold. And to help ensure that, she had to eliminate her number-one rival, Nancy Kerrigan. So, Harding and her husband, Jeff Gilooly, concocted a scheme to attack Kerrigan with a twenty-one-inch metal baton.

The attack was vicious. But Kerrigan's leg was only bruised, not broken. The injury did force Kerrigan to withdraw from the national championships. Harding won that event, and she and Kerrigan were both ultimately selected for the 1994 Olympic team. It made for some great drama when they were warming up on the ice together. Harding finished eighth in Lillehammer, while Kerrigan, by then recovered from the injury, won the silver medal behind Oksana Baiul from Ukraine.

But it was the attack itself that is etched in people's minds. Video cameras captured Kerrigan, after the attack, screaming, *"Why? Why? Why?"*

Unprovoked attacks often come out of nowhere. Because they are unexpected, no one is prepared for them. *"Why? I didn't do anything"* is often the refrain heard from victims.

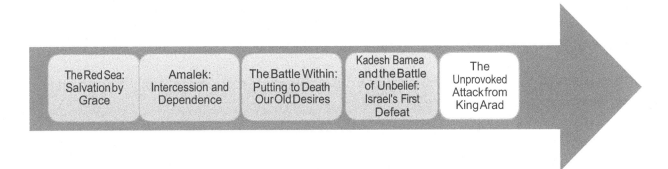

Numbers 21 records Joshua's fifth battle, the first for a new generation and army of Israel. Israel has been wandering in the wilderness for thirty-eight long years, learning (and sometimes not learning) the lessons God had for them in preparation for entering the Promised Land. And out of nowhere, an unprovoked attack occurs.

> *The king of Arad, the Canaanite, who dwelt in the South, heard that Israel was coming on the road to Atharim. Then he fought against Israel and took some of them prisoners. So Israel made a vow to the* Lord, *and said, "If You will indeed deliver this people into my hand,*

then I will utterly destroy their cities." And the Lord listened to the voice of Israel and delivered up the Canaanites, and they utterly destroyed them and their cities. So the name of that place was called Hormah. (Numbers 21:1–3)

For Joshua, this battle brought back memories from thirty-eight years earlier. He had seen Israel defeated by Amalek and the Canaanites because Israel attempted to fight in their own power. Many died that day, while those who survived ran like cowards as they were chased as far as Hormah.

Then the Amalekites and the Canaanites who dwelt in that mountain came down and attacked them, and drove them back as far as Hormah. (Numbers 14:45)

Hormah. Do you remember that city? It was mentioned in passing in Numbers 14. But Joshua never forgot it. It was like a nightmare to him, for it represented failure and a departure from God's plan of victory for His people. Instead of inheriting the Promised Land, that generation of cowards died day by day for the next thirty-eight years, until all who refused to obey God at Kadesh had died.

> *Instead of inheriting the Promised Land, that generation of cowards died day by day for the next thirty-eight years, until all who refused to obey God at Kadesh had died.*

Now their children had risen in their place with a promise from God that they would possess the Promised Land. But none of them had ever fought a war. None except Joshua and Caleb.

It is fitting that this generation's first victory came at the last place where their fathers were defeated. Would they be cowards like their fathers? Would they turn and run when their backs were against the wall? Or would they instead exercise faith and become giant-killers like Joshua and Caleb whom they now followed into battle?

This battle will go a long way in making men out of boys and produce debatably the greatest generation in the history of Israel.

God Picked the Battle and the Battlefield

Did they plan to fight here? Not at all! God led them to this memorial of defeat to change its name and memory. It would further serve as a launching pad for future victories in Canaan.

Notice, they were here by God's divine leadership and providence. They came to Edom, and Moses petitioned their king for peaceful passage. But God closed the door on their attempt to travel the King's Highway through Edom (Numbers 20:14–21).

Author E. H. Merrill says, "He [Moses] then requested permission from the king of Edom to take the famous King's Highway (20:17), a route that passed from the Red Sea (Gulf of Aqabah) north to Damascus via the Edomite city of Sela (later known as Petra). Moses appealed to Edom as a brother (v. 14), because the Edomites were descendants of Esau, Jacob's brother (cf. Gen. 36:6–8)."[14]

Follow the Bypass Signs Closely

All of us have traveled interstate highways with plans of arriving on time at our destination. Then the traffic ahead slows. Then it stops. Then you see the detour signs redirecting you in a different direction and to another road. Most of the time detours are a big interruption and a waste of time. Or so we think.

Joshua learned that God directs not only by open doors but also by closed doors. He watched Moses take a longer detour route to the Promised Land. Moses was confident in God's leadership, but this new generation had to learn to trust God. They will later complain like their fathers did when they tempted God ten times (Numbers 21:4–6).

Notice that they were attacked this time while following God's man Moses, and the Ark of the Covenant, and the Glory cloud of God. Unlike the last battle where Israel was defeated because they were in the wrong place, here they were in the right place when they were attacked.

The question before Israel was not "Are we in the right place?" but "Are we here with the right spirit of faith?" Often when we experience a surprise attack, we wonder if we have done something wrong. As believers we can be in the right place with God and still be attacked because we now belong to Christ. Sometimes the only reason you are attacked is because you belong to God and are following Him.

> *As believers we can be in the right place with God and still be attacked because we now belong to Christ. Sometimes the only reason you are attacked is because you belong to God and are following Him.*

Jesus said, *"If the world hates you, you know that it hated Me before it hated you. If you were of the world, the world would love its own. Yet because you are not of the world, but I chose you out of the world, therefore the world hates you"* (John 15:18–19). He also said, *"I have given them Your word; and the world has hated them because they are not of the world, just as I am not of the world"* (John 17:14).

---

[14] Merrill, E. H. (1985). Numbers. In J. F. Walvoord & R. B. Zuck (Eds.), *The Bible Knowledge Commentary: An Exposition of the Scriptures* (Vol. 1, p. 239). Wheaton, IL: Victor Books.

Getting Knocked Down Does Not Mean You are Knocked Out

Perhaps Arad knew about Israel's defeat thirty-eight years before. This may have added to his confidence and pride in attacking Israel. Arad's surprise attack caused confusion and a temporary defeat for Israel. Some died, and some were taken as prisoners.

This new generation of soldiers faced a critical moment. Their fathers turned back in fear and unbelief at the report of the evil spies at Kadesh. However, even though this new generation was knocked down by Arad, they turned to the Lord. *"So Israel made a vow to the Lord, and said, "If You will indeed deliver this people into my hand, then I will utterly destroy their cities."* (Numbers 21:2)

We are not told what Israel's leaders said to the soldiers to build their faith, but we can be sure that they were reminded that the same Lord who fought for them at the Red Sea would fight with them against Arad and the Canaanites.

No doubt the message of faith from Joshua and Caleb did not change. They may have reminded the young army what they said to their fathers thirty-eight years before, when they refused to believe:

> *Then Caleb quieted the people before Moses, and said, "Let us go up at once and take possession, for we are well able to overcome it...."*
>
> *But Joshua the son of Nun and Caleb the son of Jephunneh, who were among those who had spied out the land, tore their clothes; and they spoke to all the congregation of the children of Israel, saying: "The land we passed through to spy out is an exceedingly good land. If the Lord delights in us, then He will bring us into this land and give it to us, 'a land which flows with milk and honey.'*
>
> *Only do not rebel against the Lord, nor fear the people of the land, for they are our bread; their protection has departed from them, and the Lord is with us. Do not fear them."* (Numbers 13:30; 14:6–9)

You could boil Joshua's and Caleb's message of faith down to a simple challenge: "Who are you going to believe? Your fathers chose fear over faith and died in judgment. The two men who God promised would enter the Promised Land because of their faith are still here." Looking at it that way, the choice was obvious.

Remember: Getting knocked down does not mean you are knocked out.

Israel Humbled Themselves and Sought God in Their Time of Need

Not only did Israel commit to go to war against Arad and the Canaanites, but they also went further with a vow to God of utter destruction. Matthew Henry's comment here is helpful in understanding why total destruction was necessary:

94

Thus Israel here promised to destroy the cities of these Canaanites, as devoted to God, and not to take the spoil of them to their own use. If God would give them victory, he should have all the praise, and they would not make a gain of it to themselves. When we are in this frame we are prepared to receive mercy.[15]

Names of places and people in the Bible mean something. They convey a message—and the meaning of *Hormah* is quite instructive. Hormah means "utter destruction."

A vow is not unusual prior to military actions. "Utterly destroy" translates the Hebrew verb from which the noun Hormah (utter destruction) is derived. It is a consecration of the spoils of war to the Lord through total destruction.[16]

Faith Pleases God

God responded to Israel's faith and delivered up the Canaanites. In this battle, as we saw with Amalek, they were to fight with all their might but also to trust God to deliver them.

> And the LORD listened to the voice of Israel and delivered up the Canaanites, and they utterly destroyed them and their cities. So the name of that place was called Hormah. (Numbers 21:3)

Their fathers had refused to enter the Promised Land thirty-eight years earlier. However, God had a plan for Israel to take the land, led by Joshua and Caleb.

> But your little ones, whom you said would be victims, I will bring in, and they shall know the land which you have despised. (Numbers 14:31)

From this battle, we can glean some lessons for us today:

☐ Remember *who* and *what* you ran from in the past. Don't repeat that mistake. Instead, turn to God and stand in His victory. Whatever happened in the past is in the past. Even though there was failure, we can still learn from those failures and walk faithfully with God in the present.

Even though there was failure, we can still learn from those failures and walk faithfully with God in the present.

---

[15] Henry, M. (1994). *Matthew Henry's Commentary on the Whole Bible: Complete and Unabridged in One Volume* (p. 218). Peabody: Hendrickson.
[16] Hayford, J. W. (Ed.). (1997). *Spirit Filled Life Study Bible* (Electronic ed., Nu 20:29–21:4). Nashville, TN: Thomas Nelson.

☐ Detours and closed doors often lead us to greater victories. God is not limited by a detour. In fact, sometimes He engineers the detour so we will walk with Him in faith. And as we do, the journey becomes a great adventure.

☐ Just because you are attacked does not mean you are out of the will of God. It may mean that you are being led by God. Remember Jesus' promise: *"If they persecuted Me, they will persecute You. If they hated Me, they will hate You"* (John 15:18–25). You can take that as a clear promise from God, just like *"I will be with you always, even to the end of the age"* (Matthew 28:20).

Persecution isn't fun… no one likes it. But whenever the Church has been persecuted throughout history, its mission has expanded, and the Church has grown. The blood of martyrs has always been the seed of the Church. I encourage you to get a copy of *Foxe's Book of Martyrs,* which tells the story of the sufferings of Protestants under the Catholic church, with particular emphasis on England and Scotland. You will be encouraged to see God's hand of sovereignty at work, even during persecution.

☐ Just because you have lost a battle does not mean you have lost the war. God is still the God of the Second Chance. Do you remember Peter's failure when three times he denied knowing Jesus? Jesus met him after the resurrection and simply asked, *"Peter, do you love Me?"* No condemnation. No embarrassment. Only a question: *where is your heart? And Jesus restored Peter to an effective ministry.*

It's never too late to come back to Jesus. Have you failed Him? Me too. All of us have. And He welcomes us back with open arms, freely forgiving us and forever reminding us that *there is therefore now no condemnation for those who are in Christ Jesus.* You have been set free. Now live a life worthy of His love for you.

> *You have been set free. Now live a life worthy of His love for you.*

☐ We all need role models. You're going to follow somebody. It is always better to follow the examples of living faith than to follow those who run in fear. Choose your heroes carefully.

☐ Dedicate yourself and the spoils of war to God and see what God will do. Second Chronicles 16:9 reminds us, "For the eyes of the Lord range throughout the earth to strengthen those whose hearts are fully committed to him."

Discouragement: We Are Often Most Vulnerable after a Spiritual Victory

There is another great lesson from this passage that is relevant to all of us. Israel rallied after an initial defeat from Arad, and, in dependence upon God, utterly destroyed him and his cities.

Now they marched on around Edom and because the way was difficult, they became discouraged.

> *Then they journeyed from Mount Hor by the Way of the Red Sea, to go around the land of Edom; and the soul of the people became very discouraged on the way.* (Numbers 21:4)

Adrenaline from the thrill of victory can drain us emotionally. We're left empty, exhausted, and sometimes isolated. And Satan is quite ready to step in with his strategy of discouragement and depression.

When Satan cannot defeat us with an army, he often uses strategies where we defeat ourselves through the weakness of our emotions. Days with heat, sun, little water and food, and the exhaustion of battle, wore on the bodies and emotions of Israel. The joy of victory had been forgotten as they began to speak against God and Moses just as their fathers had done. Names and faces had changed from the previous generation, but the response of the flesh never changes in any generation.

> *And the people spoke against God and against Moses: "Why have you brought us up out of Egypt to die in the wilderness? For there is no food and no water, and our soul loathes this worthless bread."* (Numbers 21:5)

Discouragement defeated more soldiers than swords did in Israel. The same is true in our generation of Christian ministry. A large percentage of ministers leave the ministry every year because of the hardness of the way. Discouragement settles in and they give up the fight. The same can be said for Christian workers in our churches.

Discouragement defeated more soldiers than swords did in Israel.
The same is true in our generation of Christian ministry.

Discouragement will shrink your vision and steal your joy. Many great servants of God battled discouragement. Job cursed the day he was born. Moses asked the Lord to kill him. Elijah felt so discouraged over the spiritual apathy and idolatry of Israel that he felt all alone and prayed to die. Jonah was so discouraged he also wished for death. Jeremiah told God he would no longer speak in His name because of the rejection of the people he was sent to minister to.

> *Cursed be the day in which I was born! Let the day not be blessed in which my mother bore me! … Why did I come forth from the womb to see labor and sorrow, that my days should be consumed with shame?* (Jeremiah 20:14, 18)

Discouragement cannot be overlooked as a great enemy of the soldier of Christ. The weakness of our flesh and emotions makes us vulnerable to thoughts that will prompt us to retreat from walking by faith to walking by sight.

The battle of the mind is the stronghold that Satan desires to win. If we succumb to his whispers or his verbalizing through the mouths of people like the ten evil spies, we will be defeated. It is a wise soldier that is able to endure hardness when the way is difficult and to take command over his emotions that try to rule him. Take advantage of the opportunities for rest and refreshment that God provides. You cannot survive if you always rev your engine to the max.

Take advantage of the opportunities for rest and refreshment that God provides.
You cannot survive if you always rev your engine to the max.

Boot Camp before the Battlefield

God knew what He was doing in leading the young soldiers through a hard way. It was part of their training for the many battles they were about to face in the conquest of the seven nations of the Promised Land.

Soldiers know that if you cannot endure the harshness of boot camp, you will not be fit for the even harder environment of the battlefield. Boot camp pushes both the body and the emotions to their limits.

Consider the training of the Navy SEALS—the elite fighting force of our Armed Forces. The Seals were first commissioned by President Kennedy. According to the website Plex.page, the SEALs are "expertly trained to deliver highly specialized, intensely challenging warfare capabilities that are beyond the means of standard military forces."

The uniform didn't make these men an elite fighting machine. It was their intense training. Very few qualified for the training and of those who began the training, less than 1 percent completed it because it so difficult. The last week of their training is called "Hell week" because so few can endure the strain. The instructors are constantly pushing the young soldiers and shouting at them and reminding them that they can "Ring the bell" to signal that they quit. There is a literal bell in their training where a soldier who can no longer endure the training can ring the bell as his public declaration that he cannot endure the training any longer.

Joshua and Caleb were God's Navy SEALs. They endured the harsh training of the wilderness and were ready to lead this new generation of soldier recruits. That young generation of soldiers should have kept marching and remained silent, taking their cue from the men of faith who led them. Their fathers had not endured God's leadership in the wilderness Boot Camp, and at Kadesh they had "rung the bell" and turned back in the day of battle.

A good soldier does not murmur at the hardness of the way. He or she continues following God, trusting that everywhere the Lord leads is with purpose.

God Chastened and Gave More Grace

God quickly corrected that new generation lest they go farther down the road their fathers took: *"So the LORD sent fiery serpents among the people, and they bit the people; and many of the people of Israel died."* (Numbers 21:6)

Those who led this rebellion of complaining were destroyed by serpents. The New Testament looks at this scene and sees Christ present with them: *Nor let us tempt Christ, as some of them also tempted, and were destroyed by serpents; nor complain, as some of them also complained, and were destroyed by the destroyer* (1 Corinthians 10:9–10).

We have already seen that the rock struck in the wilderness provided a New Testament picture for us. Jesus was struck by God for our sins. The true Rock was struck and ultimately provided Living Water for us. Now we see Christ our Savior made a curse for us when He was lifted up on the Cross.

> *Therefore the people came to Moses, and said, "We have sinned, for we have spoken against the LORD and against you; pray to the LORD that He take away the serpents from us." So Moses prayed for the people. Then the LORD said to Moses, "Make a fiery serpent, and set it on a pole; and it shall be that everyone who is bitten, when he looks at it, shall live." So Moses made a bronze serpent, and put it on a pole; and so it was, if a serpent had bitten anyone, when he looked at the bronze serpent, he lived.* (Numbers 21:7–9)

God's chastening ended their rebellion. They cried out to God, confessing their sins. God's remedy of raising a bronze serpent on a pole lifted high for all to see brought healing to any who looked in faith when they were bitten by the poisonous serpent.

> *And as Moses lifted up the serpent in the wilderness, even so must the Son of Man be lifted up, that whoever believes in Him should not perish but have eternal life.* (John 3:14–15)

> *Christ has redeemed us from the curse of the law, having become a curse for us (for it is written, "Cursed is everyone who hangs on a tree."* (Galatians 3:13)

Consider the comparison:

- ☐ We also have sinned like our father Adam, and the poison of sin that brings death is in us.
- ☐ We also have rebelled against God.
- ☐ Sin brought not only a curse on the serpent but upon us as well.

- ☐ God in grace provided salvation in Christ.
- ☐ Christ who knew no sin, was made sin for us and took the curse and judgment of sin upon Himself on the Cross (2 Corinthians 5:21; Galatians 3:13).
- ☐ We are saved when we in faith look to Christ lifted up for us.

God's gracious provision is again seen as Christ. God chastened and forgave the people, and then led them on to their next battle and conquest. The simplicity of the Gospel of grace and faith can be seen with the little phrase: *"Look and Live."* Just as in the battle at the Red Sea, all we can do in salvation is to *"Stand still and see the salvation of the Lord."*

> *The simplicity of the Gospel of grace and faith can be seen with the little phrase:*
> *"Look and Live." Just as in the battle at the Red Sea, all we can do in salvation is to*
> *"Stand still and see the salvation of the Lord."*

As we conclude this chapter, here is a summary of the applications gleaned from the battle with Arad:

- ☐ We all face giants. But we must do more than conquer our fears and face the giants. We must also control our emotions and not let discouragement defeat us.

- ☐ There are long, difficult paths in our lives. These serve as part of our training for greater victories tomorrow. We must trust God in this process and know that *all things work together for good to those who love God* (Romans 8:28).

- ☐ It is better to silently follow our leaders in faith than to join the crowd of quitters who voice their emotions that lead to defeat.

- ☐ When we sin, we should confess our sin and look to God for His forgiveness in Christ.

With a victory under their belts, Israel experienced a time of God humbling them through training and chastening. Now they are ready to continue their mission of the conquest of the Promised Land.

 **Application**

Write down a couple of statements from this chapter and explain what they mean to your walk with God.

1.

2.

09   The Battles of Sihon and Og

Last Words Are Lasting Words

The last words that people ever say are often quite memorable.

- [ ] Augustus Caesar, the first Roman emperor, reportedly said to his subjects, "I found Rome of clay; I leave it to you in marble."

- [ ] Musician Bob Marley said, "Money can't buy life."

- [ ] Richard B. Mellon was a multimillionaire. He was the president of Alcoa. He and his brother Andrew had a little game of Tag going on. The weird thing was, this game of Tag lasted for like seven decades. When Richard was on his deathbed, he called his brother over and whispered, "Last tag." Poor Andrew remained "It" for four years, until he died.

- [ ] Comedian Groucho Marx said, "This is no way to live!"

- [ ] Drummer Buddy Rich died after surgery in 1987. As he was being prepped for surgery, a nurse asked him, "Is there anything you can't take?" Rich replied, "Yeah, country music."

The last words Jesus uttered were quite different. They were inspiring—a challenge to the disciples that still motivates millions today:

> *And Jesus came and spoke to them, saying, "All authority has been given to Me in heaven and on earth. Go therefore and make disciples of all the nations, baptizing them in the name of the Father and of the Son and of the Holy Spirit, teaching them to observe all things that I have commanded you; and lo, I am with you always, even to the end of the age."* (Matthew 28:18–20)

Moses also issued a deathbed challenge ... calling Joshua to be strong and courageous (Deuteronomy 31:7). He gathered all Israel together and issued a charge to Joshua as the new leader and affirmed, charged, and encouraged Joshua as he faced the conquest of Canaan: *"Be strong and of good courage ... do not fear nor be afraid of them"* (Deuteronomy 31:6).

> *Then Moses went and spoke these words to all Israel. And he said to them: "I am one hundred and twenty years old today. I can no longer go out and come in. Also the Lord has said to me, 'You shall not cross over this Jordan.' The Lord your God Himself crosses over before you; He will destroy these nations from before you, and you shall dispossess them. Joshua himself crosses over before you, just as the Lord has said. And the Lord will do to them **as He did to Sihon and Og**, the kings of the Amorites and their land, when He destroyed them.* (Deuteronomy 31:1–4, emphasis mine)

| The Red Sea: Salvation by Grace | Amalek: Intercession and Dependence | The Battle Within: Putting to Death Our Old Desires | Kadesh Barnea and the Battle of Unbelief: Israel's First Defeat | The Unprovoked Attack from King Arad | The Battle of Sihon and Og: Firstfruits |

Moses referred back to the victories over Sihon and Og as a foundational pattern and illustration for Joshua in the future. When Joshua went up to the battle of Jericho, he was to remember what God did in their victory over Sihon and Og. Remembering God's victories in the past would build his faith in the future.

Remembering always does that. Something happens when we meditate on what God has done in the past. We recognize His power, His faithfulness, His compassion, and His mercy. And we remember that what the Lord has done in the past, He will be faithful to do for us today.

What the Lord has done in the past, He will be faithful to do for us today.

God's victory over Sihon and Og inspired faith in Israel. But it caused her enemies to fear. In fact, Joshua learned at Jericho that all the nations of Canaan trembled in fear because of Israel and their God. Rahab was converted because she had heard of God's great works. But it had the opposite effect on the rest of the nations—their hearts were hardened.

> *I know that the LORD has given you the land, that the terror of you has fallen on us, and that all the inhabitants of the land are fainthearted because of you. For we have heard how the LORD dried up the water of the Red Sea for you when you came out of Egypt, and what you did to the two kings of the Amorites who were on the other side of the Jordan,* **Sihon and Og, whom you utterly destroyed.** *And as soon as we heard these things, our hearts melted.* (Joshua 2:9–11, emphasis mine)

God used the victories over Sihon and Og as a pattern to build faith in Israel for tomorrow's battles. That same principle applies to us. When God gives you victory in one area of your life against a difficult enemy or temptation, it is a pattern that He will do the same against tomorrow's difficulties.

When God gives you victory in one area of your life against a difficult enemy or temptation, it is a pattern that He will do the same against tomorrow's difficulties.

Paul made the argument that since God did the greatest thing in giving us victory through Christ's death and resurrection, then *how much more* will He work in us to give us victory over sin in our daily lives.

> *For if when we were enemies we were reconciled to God through the death of His Son, much more, having been reconciled, we shall be saved by His life.* (Romans 5:10)

When we are in our greatest battles of temptation, discouragement, or personal attacks, we need to take a Vitamin R pill—the pill that causes us to **REMEMBER!** The death of Christ is the ultimate proof of God's love and provision for us. At Jericho, Joshua looked back to all the past battles and remembered the Lord's deliverances... the Red Sea, Amalek, Arad, Sihon, Og, Balaam, and the Midianites.

> *When we are in our greatest battles of temptation, discouragement, or personal attacks, we need to take a Vitamin R" pill—the pill that causes us to **REMEMBER!***

We, too, can look back to the victory Christ won for us at the Cross. Notice how Paul connects the victory won at the Cross with the *much more* of what God promises to do for us:

> *But God demonstrates His own love toward us, in that while we were still sinners, Christ died for us.* **Much more** *then, having now been justified by His blood, we shall be saved from wrath through Him. For if when we were enemies we were reconciled to God through the death of His Son,* **much more**, *having been reconciled, we shall be saved by His life.* (Romans 5:8–10, emphasis mine)

There is a fruitful, victorious future for Israel in the Promised Land. In a similar vein, there is an abundant, victorious life that awaits each believer in their walk with Jesus.

The Battle against Sihon and Og

We now turn to the fifth and sixth battles in Joshua's preparation for the conquest of the Promised Land. These are recorded in Numbers 21:21–35 and in Deuteronomy 2:24–37, 3:1–11. God memorializes this victory by repeating it several times in Scripture. It is also mentioned several times in Joshua, Nehemiah, and the Psalms.

These two battles are grouped together in Scripture as God delivered two great kingdoms to Israel. These were the powerhouses of Sihon, king of the Amorites, and Og, king of Bashan. After the defeat of Sihon, God uses that victory as a promise of victory over Og, *"Do not fear him, for I have delivered him into your hand, with all his people and his land; and you shall do to him as you did to Sihon king of the Amorites"* (Numbers 21:34).

After the victory over King Arad, God led Israel toward the Promised Land. But war was not to be waged against any nation just because Israel desired their wealth and land. War could not be out of greed and lust to acquire the property and wealth of someone else. With Israel, war had to be as a result of a just cause.

Israel passed through three nations on their journey to their inheritance. As Israel neared these nations, God told them not to fight with those nations. God gave Mt Seir to Esau. He gave Moab and Ammon to Lot.[17]

> *Do not meddle with them, for I will not give you any of their land, no, not so much as one footstep, because I have given Mount Seir to Esau as a possession.* (Deuteronomy 2:5)

> *Then the LORD said to me [Moses], "Do not harass Moab, nor contend with them in battle, for I will not give you any of their land as a possession, because I have given Ar to the descendants of Lot as a possession."* (Deuteronomy 2:9)

> *And when you come near the people of Ammon, do not harass them or meddle with them, for I will not give you any of the land of the people of Ammon as a possession, because I have given it to the descendants of Lot as a possession.* (Deuteronomy 2:19)

Nevertheless, God expanded Israel's borders.

Even though God forbade Israel from attacking these nations, there seems to be an exception. Moab, like all the nations around the Promised Land, worshiped demon gods through idols. Their abominations even included human sacrifices. God allowed Sihon, King of the Amorites, to defeat Moab and take possession of some of its land. When Sihon went to war against Israel, they utterly destroyed Sihon's kingdom. The land once owned by Moab was given to Israel as their permanent inheritance.

> *For Heshbon was the city of Sihon king of the Amorites, who had fought against the former king of Moab, and had taken all his land from his hand as far as the Arnon.* (Numbers 21:26)

> *Rise, take your journey, and cross over the River Arnon. Look, I have given into your hand Sihon the Amorite, king of Heshbon, and his land. Begin to possess it, and engage him in battle. This day I will begin to put the dread and fear of you upon the nations under the whole heaven, who shall hear the report of you, and shall tremble and be in anguish because of you.* (Deuteronomy 2:24–25)

Obedient soldiers often receive double blessings. Later, we will see God expanded the borders of Caleb's inheritance because of his faithfulness to God.

---

[17] For a detailed study on God raising up one nation to judge another nation, see author's book, *Does God Still Judge Nations? Will God Judge America?*

The parable of the talents teaches that the one servant who received five talents and made five more talents was commended and rewarded by the Lord. The servant who took his one talent and did not increase it was reproved. His talent was taken from him and given to the one who had made five more talents for his Lord.

> *So take the talent from him, and give it to him who has ten talents. For to everyone who has, more will be given, and he will have abundance; but from him who does not have, even what he has will be taken away.* (Matthew 25:28–29)

Here is the principle God wants us to remember: When we live faithfully before the Lord, our reward will be increased.

When we live faithfully before the Lord, our reward will be increased.

An Earthly View of the Battle

When Israel came to Sihon, king of the Amorites, they sought a peaceful passage through his land.

> *Then Israel sent messengers to Sihon king of the Amorites, saying, "Let me pass through your land. We will not turn aside into fields or vineyards; we will not drink water from wells. We will go by the King's Highway until we have passed through your territory." But Sihon would not allow Israel to pass through his territory. So Sihon gathered all his people together and went out against Israel in the wilderness, and he came to Jahaz and fought against Israel. Then Israel defeated him with the edge of the sword, and took possession of his land from the Arnon to the Jabbok.* (Numbers 21:23–24)

This account only gives us an earthly, temporal view of the battle. Israel would not have fought Sihon if he had not initiated war with Israel. It seems Israel's intent was simply to pass through the land.

A Heavenly View of the Battle

However, God often gives us a panoramic view of the chessboard of heaven between God's sovereignty and man's accountability. God is always able to accomplish His will without making Himself a party to sin or making men mere robots. In Deuteronomy 2:24–25, God declared the future as though it was past tense, *"I have given into your hand Sihon and his land."*

God sees the future as if it were the present. He knows exactly what will happen and how it will come to pass. Faith is able to *call things that are not as though they were,* just because God has promised (Romans 4:17).

God sees the future as if it were the present. He knows exactly what will happen and how it will come to pass. Faith is able to call things that are not as though they were, just because God has promised (Romans 4:17).

And I sent messengers from the Wilderness of Kedemoth to Sihon king of Heshbon, with words of peace, saying, 'Let me pass through your land; I will keep strictly to the road, and I will turn neither to the right nor to the left......until I cross the Jordan to the land which the LORD our God is giving us.' But Sihon king of Heshbon would not let us pass through, for the LORD your God hardened his spirit and made his heart obstinate, that He might deliver him into your hand, as it is this day. And the LORD said to me, "See, I have begun to give Sihon and his land over to you. Begin to possess it, that you may inherit his land." Then Sihon and all his people came out against us to fight at Jahaz. And the LORD our God delivered him over to us; so we defeated him, his sons, and all his people. (Deuteronomy 2:26–33)

The promise God made to Abraham over four hundred years earlier has now to come to pass. The iniquity of the Amorites is now full. Sihon and his nation long refused the truth... and God gave them up to judgment. Sihon first hardened his own heart, and now God further hardened his heart to lead him to judgment.

During all these events, Joshua had his eyes open. He saw all that God was doing. The hardening of Sihon's heart was part of Joshua's training to prepare him for the conquest of the Promised Land.

Joshua made war a long time with all those kings. There was not a city that made peace with the children of Israel, except the Hivites, the inhabitants of Gibeon. All the others they took in battle. For it was of the LORD to harden their hearts, that they should come against Israel in battle, that He might utterly destroy them, and that they might receive no mercy, but that He might destroy them, as the LORD had commanded Moses. (Joshua 11:18–20)

God goes before us in the battle. He is sovereign over the hearts of men and women. The soldier must follow his marching orders and trust that a sovereign God can move in the hearts of people.

God goes before us in the battle. He is sovereign over the hearts of men and women. The soldier must follow his marching orders and trust that a sovereign God can move in the hearts of people.

Giants Slayers and Wall Climbers

God emphasized how large the bed of King Og was. It measured six feet wide by thirteen and a half feet long (Deuteronomy 3:11). He must have been a giant!

The generation of soldiers who followed Joshua in the conquest of the Promised Land faced the fears of their fathers' generation. Their fathers saw giants and fortified cities with high walls and, because of unbelief, missed the Promised Land. Before Joshua led these new soldiers against the high walls of Jericho, God let them face giants and walled cities with Sihon and Og.

The Lord was also specific about sixty fortified cities with high walls that this new generation of soldiers did not run from as their fathers did: *All these cities were fortified with high walls, gates, and bars, besides a great many rural towns* (Deuteronomy 3:5).

The question before this new generation was, "Are you going to be like your fathers and respond to giants and fortified walls with fear and unbelief, or will you trust the promises of God that He will lead you to victory?" Their fathers had said,

> *"Nevertheless the people who dwell in the land are strong; the cities are fortified and very large; moreover we saw the descendants of Anak there. There we saw the giants (the descendants of Anak came from the giants); and we were like grasshoppers in our own sight, and so we were in their sight."* (Numbers 13:28, 33)

Instead, this new generation believed the promises of God. They followed the example of Moses, Joshua, and Caleb. The words of Caleb could still be heard by this new generation: *"Let us go up at once and take possession, for we are well able to overcome it"* (Numbers 13:30).

What a powerful, living witness Joshua and Caleb were to this new generation! Their fathers were dead because of fear and unbelief, but Joshua and Caleb lived on to lead them to the conquest and inheritance they were promised.

Every one of us has people we respect and model our lives after. Some people are swayed by the crowd and influenced by them. The result is *always* regret, heartache, and disappointment. It is always better to follow living men of faith than to memorialize the unbelief of dead fathers.

---

*It is always better to follow living men of faith
than to memorialize the unbelief of dead fathers.*

Sacrifice and Reward

You pay a price as a soldier. When duty calls, you forsake everything to follow orders. You are often away from loved ones for many months at a time. Some soldiers miss their child's first steps, their son's first ball game, their daughter's graduation, or weddings of close family and friends.

That was true in ancient times as well. Soldiers from the tribes of Reuben, Gad, and half tribe of Manasseh left their wives and children in the land taken from Sihon and Og. Forty thousand of them crossed the Jordan River, going before Israel and receiving the first wave of attacks from the enemy. They were away from their families for seven long years. This required great sacrifice and bold faith.

As one nation, the twelve tribes of Israel defeated both Sihon and Og. The land they took was fruitful and abundant. It was perfect for grazing hundreds of thousands of cattle and sheep. Reuben, Gad, and half of the tribe of Manasseh requested that Moses give them this land to the east of the Jordan River as their inheritance.

> *Therefore they said, "If we have found favor in your sight, let this land be given to your servants as a possession. Do not take us over the Jordan."* (Numbers 32:6–8)

At first, Moses misinterpreted their request as a refusal to fight with their brethren. He thought back to how the previous generation fearfully refused to cross the Jordan and remembered its deadly result to all of Israel.

> *And Moses said to the children of Gad and to the children of Reuben: **"Shall your brethren go to war while you sit here?** Now why will you discourage the heart of the children of Israel from going over into the land which the LORD has given them? Thus your fathers did when I sent them away from Kadesh Barnea to see the land.* (Numbers 32:6–8, emphasis mine)

Moses was well acquainted with the sacrifices of war. It was not right for some to go to war and sacrifice while others sat and enjoyed rest. Enjoying our life and possessions is proper in normal times, but not in time of war. Draft dodgers and deserters often faced the death penalty as motivation for soldiers to stay firm in their commitment and keep a unified army.

 **Application**

God compares the church to a body that is made up of many parts. Every member has a function and service to the whole body. And yet many people sit on the sidelines, enjoying rest, while others serve and face battles. Someone said, "Ten percent of the church serves and does ninety percent of the work, while ninety percent does nothing." I have found that servants of Christ grow weary when they give so much and see other Christians giving so little. Paul's words to Timothy speak to this issue:

> *You therefore must endure hardship as a good soldier of Jesus Christ. No one engaged in warfare entangles himself with the affairs of this life, that he may please him who enlisted him as a soldier.* (2 Timothy 2:3–4)

Sacrifice Illustrated

Moses soon realized that Reuben, Gad, and the half tribe of Manasseh did not have a deserter's heart. They were champions. They proposed to go before Israel into battle and to leave their families and possessions to fight with their brethren until all the tribes received their inheritance. They would be on the battlefield for seven years before they returned to their families.

Moses agreed with their proposal and gave them as their inheritance the land conquered from King Sihon and King Og upon the condition that they were faithful to their promise:

> *Then I commanded you at that time, saying: 'The LORD your God has given you this land to possess. All you men of valor shall cross over armed before your brethren, the children of Israel. But your wives, your little ones, and your livestock (I know that you have much livestock) shall stay in your cities which I have given you, until the LORD has given rest to your brethren as to you, and they also possess the land which the LORD your God is giving them beyond the Jordan. Then each of you may return to his possession which I have given you.* (Deuteronomy 3:18–20)

These soldiers did not stay home. They forsook all and followed Joshua into battle. Their answer to Moses' question, *"Shall your brethren go to war while you sit here?"* was unequivocal. They committed to stand on the front lines of the battle and encourage their brethren.

*They committed to stand on the front lines of the battle
and encourage their brethren.*

 **Application**

Jesus calls us to forsake everything and follow Him. *"So likewise, whoever of you does not forsake all that he has cannot be My disciple"* (Luke 14:33).

This language of sacrifice is foreign to the selfish Christian who only followed Christ to have his sins forgiven and be assured of heaven when he died. With maturity comes accountability and responsibility. Consider this contrast in the following New Testament passages:

I write to you, little children, because your sins are forgiven you for His name's sake. I have written to you, young men, because you are strong, and the word of God abides in you, and you have overcome the wicked one. (1 John 2:12, 14)

*And I, brethren, could not speak to you as to spiritual people but as to carnal, as to **babes in Christ**. I fed you with milk and not with solid food; for until now you **were not able to receive it**, and even now you are still not able; for you are still carnal. For where there are envy, strife, and divisions among you, **are you not carnal and behaving like mere men?*** (1 Corinthians 3:1–3, emphasis mine)

For I have no one like-minded, who will sincerely care for your state. For all seek their own, not the things which are of Christ Jesus. (Philippians 2:20, emphasis mine)

Paul's deep love for Christ was seen by his great passion for the church and for the lost. As a good soldier, he knew the sacrifice and suffering of following Christ.

Just as I also please all men in all things, not seeking my own profit, but the profit of many, that they may be saved … Imitate me, just as I also imitate Christ. (1 Corinthians 10:33; 11:1, emphasis mine)

Paul's deep love for Christ was seen by his great passion for the church and for the lost.

How is your deep love demonstrated to others?

It is almost embarrassing today to ask ourselves if we know what it means to be a good soldier of Christ. So many people come to Christ today because of what He can offer *them*. But they fail to see the cost required of truly following Jesus. But this isn't only a twenty-first century problem. It is a human-heart problem. Jesus addressed it head-on when He said,

Now great multitudes went with Him. And He turned and said to them, "If anyone comes to Me and does not hate his father and mother, wife and children, brothers and sisters, yes, and his own life also, he cannot be My disciple. And whoever does not bear his cross and come after Me cannot be My disciple.

For which of you, intending to build a tower, does not sit down first and count the cost, whether he has enough to finish it—lest, after he has laid the foundation, and is not able to finish, all who see it begin to mock him, saying, 'This man began to build and was not able to finish'? Or what king, going to make war against another king, does not sit down first and consider whether he is able with ten thousand to meet him who comes against him with twenty thousand? Or else, while the other is still a great way off, he sends a delegation and asks conditions of peace.

So likewise, whoever of you does not forsake all that he has cannot be My disciple. (Luke 14:25–33)

Let's be honest. There is always a cost to following Jesus. Take a moment and reflect: What are the sacrifices you've had to make in following Jesus? Write them down in the space provided.

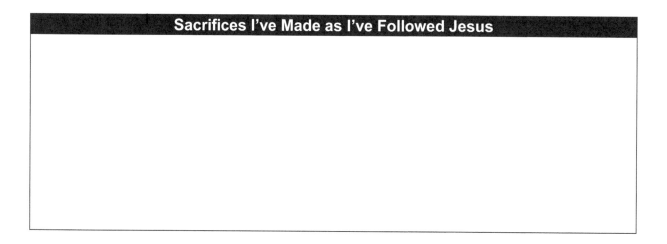

Sacrifices I've Made as I've Followed Jesus

By the way, if you're having a hard time thinking of something to write down, maybe you've been skirting your responsibilities to follow Him sacrificially.

After the soldier's sacrifice, comes great reward. After seven years of hard-fought battles, these soldiers returned to their families.

*Then Joshua called the Reubenites, the Gadites, and half the tribe of Manasseh, and said to them: "You have kept all that Moses the servant of the LORD commanded you, and have obeyed my voice in all that I commanded you. You have not left your brethren these many days, up to this day, but have kept the charge of the commandment of the LORD your God, "Return with much riches to your tents, with very much livestock, with silver, with gold, with bronze, with iron, and with very much clothing. Divide the spoil of your enemies with your brethren." * (Joshua 22:1–3, 8)

These faithful soldiers did not return empty-handed. They not only received the Lord's approval and Joshua's honor, but they were made rich and were able to enrich others.

 **Application**

This is the same pattern for us today. God is a rewarder. It is in His good nature. Some of our rewards are spiritual. Some are physical. Some are received now, and some are waiting for us in heaven. Here are a few of the Bible's promises of reward:

- ☐ When we are persecuted, there is great reward in heaven (Matthew 5:12).
- ☐ Charitable deeds will be rewarded in heaven (Matthew 6:1).
- ☐ Secret prayer will be rewarded openly (Matthew 6:6).
- ☐ Helping God's servants will be rewarded (Matthew 10:40–42).
- ☐ When Jesus returns, He comes rewarding His servants according to their works (Matthew 16:27).
- ☐ He who plants and he who waters in building God's kingdom will be rewarded according to their labor (1 Corinthians 3:8).
- ☐ All our works are tested by fire to prove our motives, and all that endures the fire will be rewarded (1 Corinthians 3:9–15).

This should inspire us to live the words of Colossians 3:23–24: *And whatever you do, do it heartily, as to the Lord and not to men, knowing that from the Lord you will receive the reward of the inheritance; for you serve the Lord Christ.*

A Personal Story

When Connie and I left our families to start a mission effort 2,600 miles away, Matthew 19:29 spoke deeply to our hearts.

> *And everyone who has left houses or brothers or sisters or father or mother or wife or children or lands, for My name's sake, shall receive a hundredfold, and inherit eternal life.* (Matthew 19:29)

It was hard leaving family and friends. It was tough going from familiar surroundings in south Louisiana and adjusting to a totally unfamiliar culture. But it was worth it. It is always worth it to follow Jesus, no matter what the sacrifice. I can say that since that day, God has continually added to our family: fathers, mothers, brothers, and sisters and we are blessed a hundredfold.

It is always worth it to follow Jesus, no matter what the sacrifice.

113

Let's conclude with a few questions:

☐ What do you believe God is calling you to do right now?

☐ What are the sacrifices that might be required as you follow Him?

☐ What are any hesitations you may be experiencing as you seek to do His will?

Be ready to answer God's call of deeper maturity. Grow up in Christ from being a baby who is cared for and become a soldier who cares for others and advances God's kingdom.

When God sends you, He will care for what you have entrusted to Him.

When God sends you, He will care for what you have entrusted to Him.

 **Application**

Amplify one statement from this chapter and try to make it personal.

10   The Unseen Battle—Part 1

When You Can't See the Enemy

He hid in caves and mountains of Afghanistan. He plotted a secret attack against the USA. While we carried on our normal comfortable lives, he recruited, trained, and indoctrinated secret soldiers who were willing to die to complete their mission of terror. All the while, we were unaware that the greatest terrorist attack in US history was coming.

Osama bin Laden secretly planted the terrorists among us. They went to flight schools in South Florida. They kept a low profile while they trained and plotted to seize commercial jets while in flight and fly them as suicide bombs into the Twin Towers, the Pentagon, and the White House.

An article in *The Palm Beach Post* reminded area residents that twelve of the nineteen terrorists lived among us as they secretly planned the 911 attacks on America.

They shopped at Target, Winn-Dixie, Office Depot, and Lowe's. They rented homes in Boynton Beach, Del Ray Beach, and Coral Springs—all of which are only a few minutes from my home. Like many area residents, I have wondered, *Did I cross their paths? Were we in the same stores or restaurants?*

What if we had known of their secret plot against us? Could we have stopped it? Could we have made a difference? Just because we cannot see the enemy or the danger doesn't mean that it is not real.

It seems that Osama bin Laden and Balaam had much in common. They both loved power, money, women, and presented themselves as worshipers of God with a righteous cause.

---

*Just because we cannot see the enemy or the danger
doesn't mean that it is not real.*

The Red Sea: Salvation by Grace	Amalek: Intercession and Dependence	The Battle Within: Putting to Death Our Old Desires	Kadesh Barnea and the Battle of Unbelief: Israel's First Defeat	The Unprovoked Attack from King Arad	The Battle of Sihon and Og: Firstfruits	The Unseen Battle

The Unseen Battle behind Enemy Lines

Israel was in a very good place. They endured forty years of wilderness travel from Egypt to the Promised Land. They experienced God fighting with them as they defeated two great nations of the Amorites. With the defeat of these two great kings came their first division of land. Reuben, Gad, and the half-tribe of Manasseh could see and touch their inheritance. There must have been great joy in the camp of Israel as they camped not far from what was supposed to be their next great victory at Jericho.

But while they worshiped God, an unseen enemy was plotting their destruction.

A false prophet by the name of Balaam was trying to curse Israel. A powerful soothsayer known for his power with the gods, he was hired by Balak, the king of Moab, to curse Israel. Balak told the prophet, "I cannot defeat them with the sword. But I know you are able to bring curses on them."

> *Then the children of Israel moved, and camped in the plains of Moab on the side of the Jordan across from Jericho. Now Balak the son of Zippor saw all that Israel had done to the Amorites. And Moab was exceedingly afraid…. Then he sent messengers to Balaam…. Therefore, please come at once, curse this people for me … for I know that he whom you bless is blessed, and he whom you curse is cursed."* (Numbers 22:1–6)

Israel was going about life as normal, completely unaware that God and Satan were at war.

Joshua learned that a greater, unseen battle between God and Satan exists behind every physical battle on earth. This experience with Balaam was certainly part of Joshua's preparation for the greater battles just before him in the conquest of the seven nations of Canaan.

Joshua learned that a greater, unseen battle between God and Satan exists behind every physical battle on earth.

116

Considering God gives four chapters to this behind-the-scenes spiritual battle (Numbers 22–25), it must have an important place in our training to be good soldiers of Jesus Christ.

Lessons on Spiritual Warfare

There are many important lessons for us to learn about spiritual warfare in our study of Numbers 22–25 and the life of Balaam.

☐ God is fighting for us even when we are not aware of secret attacks against us. There is an unseen warfare going on that we are oblivious to. This is why we need to walk step-by-step in the power of the Holy Spirit. We need His leadership and protection from those things of which we are unaware.

> *God is fighting for us even when we are not aware of secret attacks against us.*

How do we do that? Start with prayer. Express your complete dependence on Him. One of the requests in The Lord's Prayer is *lead us not into temptation.* We can't see where the temptation is. But God knows. And when we pray, we're asking Him to guide us in paths where we cannot see the dangers.

☐ Satan is a defeated foe. However, he still walks around like a roaring lion, seeking whom he may devour (1 Peter 5:8). But God sets the limits on Satan and no child of God can be touched without His permission (see Job 1).

☐ God will not allow Satan to curse that which He has blessed. Jesus was made a curse for us that we might be made new in Christ. Second Corinthians 5:21 says, *For He made Him who knew no sin to be sin for us, that we might become the righteousness of God in Him.* It's **the great exchange:** Jesus takes our sin and curse on Himself, and we receive all His righteousness in our lives. We're forgiven, set free, guaranteed eternal life, and possessors of the Holy Spirit. It's all by grace. And God gets all the glory.

> *It's **the great exchange:** Jesus takes our sin and curse on Himself, and we receive all His righteousness in our lives. We're forgiven, set free, guaranteed eternal life, and possessors of the Holy Spirit. It's all by grace. And God gets all the glory.*

☐ Our position in Christ is secure. When we come to Christ, we receive Him as Savior and Lord. And God adopts us as His children into His forever family.

☐ At this point, we might think the battle is over. But it is not. Satan cannot win the war against us, but we can, by sin, give Satan access to our flesh and allow him to defeat us from within. That is why Paul said, *Do not give the devil an opportunity* (Ephesians 4:27). Don't ignore the battle. Don't forget that Satan still seeks to destroy (John 10:10). Continue to fight the good fight.

Balaam could not curse God's covenant people, but he taught Balak how he could defeat them—not with a sword but with the seduction of women. The tempter tempted God's people … and they fell for it.

Joshua learned that God would not allow Satan to curse that which God had blessed. As long as Israel stayed in God's will, they were victorious and secure. However, when they walked in sin, they could be defeated.

God would not allow Satan to curse that which God had blessed.
As long as Israel stayed in God's will, they were victorious and secure.
However, when they walked in sin, they could be defeated.

The Enemy Who Looked Like a Friend

In these chapters, from the outward appearance, it seemed that Balaam believed in God, spoke for God, and sought to obey God. He used the covenant name of the *LORD* several times when he spoke of God. But he didn't speak for God.

Balak sent representatives with the rewards of divination to Balaam to ask him to curse Israel:

And God said to Balaam, "You shall not go with them; you shall not curse the people, for they are blessed." So Balaam rose in the morning and said to the princes of Balak, "Go back to your land, for the LORD has refused to give me permission to go with you." (Numbers 22:12–13)

Balak sent word to Balaam a second time, with more honorable representatives and more wealth, and the false prophet seemed to choose God over gold:

Then Balaam answered and said to the servants of Balak, "Though Balak were to give me his house full of silver and gold, I could not go beyond the word of the LORD my God, to do less or more. Now therefore, please, you also stay here tonight, that I may know what more the LORD will say to me." And God came to Balaam at night and said to him, "If the men come to call you, rise and go with them; but only the word which I speak to you—that you shall do." So Balaam rose in the morning, saddled his donkey, and went with the princes of Moab. (Numbers 22:18–21)

Balaam's mouth said, "I choose God over gold," and he seemed to be sincere. But God knew his heart.

Many have wondered why God stood in Balaam's way as an adversary when it was God who told him to go. *Then God's anger was aroused because he went, and the Angel of the LORD took His stand in the way as an adversary against him* (Numbers 22:22).

Balaam's response to God's drawn sword was what appeared to be humility and remorse:

> *And Balaam said to the Angel of the LORD, "I have sinned, for I did not know You stood in the way against me. Now therefore, if it displeases You, I will turn back."* (Numbers 22:34)

Was it a godly sorrow that leads to repentance, or was it the sorrow of this world that leads to death? (2 Corinthians 7:10).

Balaam was not the first nor last false professor to cry out to God, *"I have sinned."*

> "On at least eight separate occasions in the Scriptures, an individual has been forced to utter these three tragic but true words, "I have sinned." See also: Pharaoh (Ex 9:27; 10:16); Achan (Josh 7:20); Saul (1 Sam 26:21); David (2 Sam 12:13; 24:10); Job (Job 7:20); Judas (Mt 27:4); and the prodigal son (Lk 15:21). A double tragedy is seen here; for out of eight confessions, it would seem that only three (David, Job, and the prodigal son) really meant it and experienced the forgiveness of God!" [18]

Balaam's Unrighteousness and Hypocrisy Exposed

Balaam's mouth said, "I choose God over gold." It sounded right. He sounded sincere. But God saw that his heart said, "I choose gold over God."

God's own commentary on Balaam gives us the true motive of his heart. Balaam is seen as a warning against religious false prophets, and those who love power, women, and money over God. The New Testament picks up on this treachery. Three times its writers pick up the name of Balaam and use it to describe unbelievable deception. They speak of *The Way of Balaam, The Error of Balaam,* and *The Doctrine of Balaam.*

The Way of Balaam

Second Peter 2:15–16 says, *They have forsaken the right way and gone astray, following **the way of Balaam** the son of Beor, who loved the wages of unrighteousness; but he was rebuked for his iniquity: a dumb donkey speaking with a man's voice restrained the madness of the prophet.*

---

[18] Hindson, E. E., & Kroll, W. M. (Eds.). (1994). *KJV Bible Commentary* (p. 297). Nashville: Thomas Nelson.

Notice the words associated with Balaam: *forsaken the right way, loved the wages of unrighteousness*, and *the madness of the prophet*. The Way of Balaam is the way of choosing covetousness over God's true righteousness.

The Error of Balaam

Jude 11 states, *Woe to them! For they have gone in the way of Cain, have run greedily in the* **error of Balaam** *for profit, and perished in the rebellion of Korah.*

One aspect about the Error of Balaam is to know the will of God and outwardly profess it, while secretly trying to change it.

The Doctrine of Balaam

Revelation 2:14 says, *But I have a few things against you, because you have there those who hold* **the doctrine of Balaam**, *who taught Balak to put a stumbling block before the children of Israel, to eat things sacrificed to idols, and to commit sexual immorality.*

Notice that not only did Balaam love the wages of unrighteousness that Balak offered him, but he also taught Balak how to entice Israel to sin against God through temptations. He acted as Satan's agent to entice Israel's young soldiers through the flesh: wine, women, and song that led to sacrifices to idols.

The Doctrine of Balaam broadens the view of God to make God tolerant of our weakness. It turns the grace of God into tolerance for sin. It is a spirit of acceptance based upon our humanity and not upon our conformity to Christ's character.

A closer look at what the Scripture says about Balaam identifies him as a **soothsayer** that Israel killed in their revenge attack against him and Balak.

> *The children of Israel also killed with the sword Balaam the son of Beor, the soothsayer, among those who were killed by them.* (Joshua 13:22)

God said Balaam's way was **perverse** and that he used **enchantments**, which were a demonic and occultist practice that God called an abomination.

God was overriding the **secret wicked desires** of Balaam to curse Israel by substituting His blessings for Balaam's cursing.

> God says, *"But I would not listen to Balaam; therefore he continued to bless you. So I delivered you out of his hand."* (Joshua 24:10)

Learn from the Betrayers

The name Balaam becomes synonymous with deception. During the ministry of Jesus, it was the Pharisees who brought oppression and deception upon the people. There are many lessons we can learn from Balaam and his religious brothers, the Pharisees, who sought to curse Jesus.

We must beware of religious wolves that come to us as harmless sheep. Their objective is to deceive and devour. Not all religious leaders represent God. Not all religious leaders have your best interests at heart. There are those who are "of God" and there are those who are "not of God."

Remember the religious leaders of Israel during Jesus' time, who appeared to be righteous? They blessed God with their lips, but cursed Christ in their hearts. They claimed God as their father, but Jesus said that their father was the Devil (John 8:44). He also said they appeared to have washed the cup on the outside to make it clean, but within it was still full of filth and deadness (Matthew 23:25). They never dealt with the heart-problem.

And then there was Judas. Judas was like Balaam, as he experienced the knowledge and power of God, but he was a thief in his heart. Satan entered him and used him to betray Christ.

Please note this warning: It is possible to be around great works of God without knowing God. It is possible to walk with others who experience intimacy with Christ without experiencing it yourself. It is possible to look good on the outside, while being completely lost on the inside. Judas did it for three years.

> *It is possible to be around great works of God without knowing God. It is possible to walk with others who experience intimacy with Christ without experiencing it yourself. It is possible to look good on the outside, while being completely lost on the inside. Judas did it for three years.*

Balaam's Curses Turned to Prophetic Blessings by God

It seems strange that God would use a soothsayer to bless Israel and foretell of the coming of Christ. Our text shows God's sovereign power to have even a dumb donkey to speak His word. It seems to me that Balaam's covetous heart wanted to curse Israel, but God controlled each word of his four prophecies.

> *But I would not listen to Balaam; therefore he continued to bless you. So I delivered you out of his hand.* (Joshua 24:10)

In the movie *Liar, Liar* comedian Jim Carrey plays a fast-talking attorney who is known for lying even to his family and son. As his brokenhearted son blows out the candles on his birthday cake, he makes a wish that his dad could not tell a lie for the next twenty-four hours. His wish is granted. A strange force comes over Carrey. Carrey's facial expressions shows the battle he has as he tries to lie, but out of his mouth comes "the truth, the whole truth, and nothing but the truth." No matter how hard he wants to frame his words to lie to benefit himself, the truth comes out against his will.

That's exactly what happened to Balaam. God does not make us puppets, but He can accomplish His will even with unwilling vessels.

> *God did not make these prophets immoral, covetous, and liars. They already were and God allowed a lying spirit to deceive them according to their own character. The appearance of the **God** of Israel to unbelieving prophets and kings was not unique to Balaam. God revealed himself to Abimelech king of Gerar in Abraham's time (Gen. 20:6–7), to a Pharaoh in dreams (Gen. 41:25), to Nebuchadnezzar in a dream and visions (Dan. 4:1–18), and to others. As the sovereign God He rules and overrules in prophetic revelation as well as in all other areas of life. He therefore accommodated Himself to the crass manipulations of an Amorite diviner, though in the end God showed Himself to be the divine "Manipulator.[19]*

God's will cannot be thwarted. Although Satan may appear to win a skirmish or two, God is sovereign over everything. Nothing happens that He does not control.

God's will cannot be thwarted.
Although Satan may appear to win a skirmish or two,
God is sovereign over everything. Nothing happens that He does not control.

Take a moment to write down what is going on in your life right now. Make a spiritual affirmation that God is sovereign over all that you are going through. He is in control. And because He is sovereign, we can trust Him.

In the next chapter, we will continue with our study of Balaam's words and actions and see how they relate to our spiritual warfare.

[19] Merrill, E. H. (1985). Numbers. In J. F. Walvoord & R. B. Zuck (Eds.), *The Bible Knowledge Commentary: An Exposition of the Scriptures* (Vol. 1, p. 241). Wheaton, IL: Victor Books.

Introduction

Balaam spoke four oracles where he revealed God's Word. Balak offered him a lot of money to speak falsely. Balaam used enchantments to stir up the gods. But God came to him and spoke His word of truth. And that is what prevailed. We will look at just a few samplings of these oracles and relate them to our spiritual warfare.

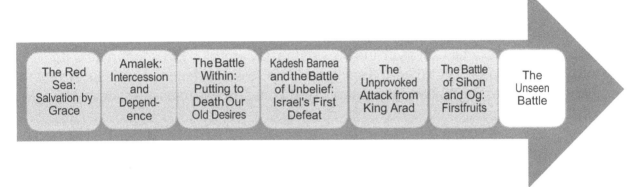

Satan Cannot Curse That Which God Has Blessed

And he took up his oracle and said: "Balak the king of Moab has brought me from Aram, from the mountains of the east. 'Come, curse Jacob for me, and come, denounce Israel!' "How shall I curse whom God has not cursed? And how shall I denounce whom the LORD has not denounced?…Behold, I have received a command to bless; He has blessed, and I cannot reverse it. (Numbers 23:7–8, 20)

While Joshua and Israel were unaware of Balak's attempt to pay Balaam for cursing Israel, God defended them. God was at war with Satan on Israel's behalf. And one of our greatest promises to remember is that Satan cannot curse that which God has blessed.

Satan cannot curse that which God has blessed.

Why can't Satan curse us, and what is the basis for our blessing? Israel's blessing was rooted in the promise God made to Abraham. Paul made it clear that the promise God made to Abraham was ultimately to Abraham's seed, Christ.

Now to Abraham and his Seed were the promises made. He does not say, "And to seeds," as of many, but as of one, "And to your Seed," who is Christ. (Galatians 3:16)

*Christ has redeemed us from the curse of the law, **having become a curse for us** (for it is written, "Cursed is everyone who hangs on a tree"), that the **blessing of Abraham** might come upon the Gentiles in Christ Jesus, that we might receive the promise of the Spirit through faith.* (Galatians 3:13–14 emphasis mine)

This is another foundational truth for soldiers of Christ to remember. Satan once had cause to curse us because of our sin. But Jesus took our sin on the Cross and became a curse for us. Now we are blessed in Christ, and Satan has no legal ground for cursing that which Christ has blessed. As redeemed children of God, we have been blessed by God to the ultimate degree:

Blessed be the God and Father of our Lord Jesus Christ, who has blessed us with every spiritual blessing in the heavenly places in Christ. (Epheisans 1:3)

What does this mean for us today? It means we can have complete confidence in Christ's victory over Satan. Christ's victory on the Cross is the basis for all our victories over Satan. Satan can only act as a bully to bluff the soldier of Christ to walk in fear and not faith. We stand in our victory, confessing that we cannot be cursed because we are blessed once and for all in Christ.

Our Lord Jesus defeated our enemy Satan and stripped him of his authority over us. I glean from an old story that helped me many years ago.

> A cruel ship captain made the lives of his sailors miserable. He ruled by pain and fear. Word arrived that the owner of the ship had stripped him of all his authority. However, the cruel captain ignored the owner's authority and continued to bark out orders to a fearful crew. Finally, one young sailor understood that the captain no longer had authority over him and stood up to him and called his bluff. At that moment the entire crew realized that they too were free from his tyranny.

At some point each of us will have to call Satan's bluff and stand up to him in our victory in Christ.

Satan Cannot Change Our Position and Standing in Christ

We are holy, righteous, and redeemed because of our identity in Christ. It was said of Israel, *(God) has not observed iniquity in Jacob, nor has He seen wickedness in Israel. The LORD his God is with him* (Numbers 23:21).

How can that be true? With all their murmuring, idolatry, and disobedience, Israel was anything but holy. In what sense can we understand that God did not see their sin? This marvelous truth is understood in the ***imputed righteousness of Christ.*** Paul wrote of believers in the first century, *For He made Him who knew no sin to be sin for us, that we might become **the righteousness of God in Him*** (2 Corinthians 5:21).

Neither Abraham nor David were perfect men. They knew their share of wickedness. God saw their wickedness and made provision for their sin just as He sees our sinful wickedness and makes provision for it in Christ.

> *God saw their wickedness and made provision for their sin*
> *just as He sees our sinful wickedness and makes provision for it in Christ.*

None of us are righteous in our own merit, but by faith in God's provision, we know both forgiveness from the penalty of sin and the righteousness of Christ imputed to us by faith.

For what does the Scripture say? "Abraham believed God, and it was accounted to him for righteousness." Now to him who works, the wages are not counted as grace but as debt. But to him who does not work but believes on Him who justifies the ungodly, his faith is accounted for righteousness, just as David also describes the blessedness of the man to whom God imputes righteousness apart from works: "Blessed are those whose lawless deeds are forgiven, and whose sins are covered; blessed is the man to whom the LORD shall not impute sin." (Romans 4:3–8)

For as by one man's disobedience many were made sinners, so also by one Man's obedience many will be made righteous. (Romans 5:19)

> *None of us are righteous in our own merit, but by faith in God's provision,*
> *we know both forgiveness from the penalty of sin*
> *and the righteousness of Christ imputed to us by faith.*

Too many believers have never heard the term, "our positional standing in Christ." They are unaware of our new identity in Him and its implications for us in our daily lives. Our standing in Christ is the truth that God looks at us no longer as sinners, but as forgiven sons and daughters. He no longer sees us in Adam but in Christ.

The soldier must understand that nothing can take him out of Christ and that the perfect righteousness of Christ imputed to him by faith alone can never be taken away from him.

Satan's tactic is to tempt us to sin by diminishing the character and holiness of God. We rationalize and diminish the seriousness of sin until we yield to the flesh. Once we yield to the flesh, Satan's tactic often changes to condemnation. He tells us that God will not forgive us and restore us to fellowship without a religious works process. This condemnation often turns our eyes away from Christ's provision in grace and as we look at ourselves, we put ourselves back under the Law.

One of Satan's strongest weapons against us is condemnation. For example, at my first church I was excited to see the spiritual growth of a young farmer who had prayed to receive Christ with me a few weeks before. At one service, I asked if anyone had a testimony to share, and the farmer went to the pulpit and made a bold but prideful statement, "I will never smoke again." I wished he had not placed so much emphasis on his own ability, and I had never asked him to stop smoking.

I did not see him in church the next Sunday and went to visit him. He told me that he could never come back to church again. I asked why? "Preacher, after I made that statement from the pulpit, I had the strongest urge to smoke. I went to my car and smoked a cigarette before I left church. I then had this thought: *You are such a hypocrite. You can never show your face in this church again.*"

I tried to explain that he was under an attack of condemnation from Satan who wanted to take him out of church. Sad to say, I never could get him to understand and return to church.

Satan Tempts and Seeks to Condemn

Temptation can come in many forms.

The enemy whispers to us, "You're a failure as a Christian. The church expects too much of you. You'll never be able to live up to their standards. Get away from them. Leave the church. Maybe come back when you get your life back together." Or he might say, "If your mate was more affectionate toward you, you wouldn't have to turn to someone else for attention."

And with that temptation comes condemnation. We see ourselves as failures, unable to live up to God's righteous standards. But the Gospel says, "That's the point! You **can't** live up to the standard. That's why you need a Savior."

Jesus did not come to be a role model for us. He came to be a sacrifice, paying the price for our sin that we could not pay. And in exchange, He gives us His righteousness as a free gift of grace. When we understand that God sees us in Christ's righteousness alone as our unchangeable position, it takes the rod of condemnation out of Satan's hand that seeks to drive us from God. We also better understand the rod of chastening in our heavenly Father's hand that draws us back to His loving side.

> When we understand that God sees us in Christ's righteousness alone as our unchangeable position, it takes the rod of condemnation out of Satan's hand that seeks to drive us from God. We also better understand the rod of chastening in our heavenly Father's hand that draws us back to His loving side.

The true believer wants to walk in personal righteousness because of Christ's perfect righteousness imputed to Him. What God worked in us, we now seek to work out of us by yielding to the indwelling Holy Spirit (Philippians 2:12–13).

In contrast, those who have made a false profession of faith will react in one of two ways. Either they will abuse the grace of God and justify a habitual walk in unrighteousness, claiming that the imputed righteousness of God covers their bad behavior, or they will strive to make up for their sins by dedication and obedience to the law through their own works.

Satan Sets Snares

A snare is a trap. The simplicity of a snare is to use the natural appetites of your victims against them to catch them by diversion. I built my first snare when I was a six-year-old child. The birds in our trees were perfectly safe from my devious plan as long as they stayed in the trees. They could fly, but I could not. But when they landed in my yard, they became my prey.

However, my dad told me how to build a snare. It only required four simple elements—a box, a stick to hold one end of the box off the ground, a long string tied to the end of the stick, and breadcrumbs to bait the snare.

I hid out of sight. I had everything in place. The trail of breadcrumbs would lead the unsuspecting bird to the greater pile of breadcrumbs under the box.

As I hid from sight, the birds left their safe refuge of the trees and landed in my yard. I watched as one bird followed my baited trail enjoying every bite until it was feasting on its prize under my box. I pulled hard on the string—out came the stick, down came the box, and the bird was now my captive.

Satan is in the snare-trapping business. He uses our natural appetites of the flesh to entice us with temptations. James says, *But each one is tempted when he is drawn away by his own desires and enticed* (James 1:14).

> *Satan is in the snare-trapping business.*
> *He uses our natural appetites of the flesh to entice us with temptations.*

God warned Israel through Moses four times not to be seduced and snared by their pagan ways (Exodus 23:33, 34:12; Deuteronomy 7:16, 26). But Satan laid the breadcrumbs of temptation with women, wine, sensual music, and dance. Then he pulled the string, and Israel was snared as they sacrificed to the demon god of Moab. Twenty-four thousand of Israel's soldiers fell into that trap and were later judged by God.

Balaam Taught Balak How to Ensnare Israel

Balaam tried to curse Israel, but God turned his curses into blessings. Not only was Israel unaware of the Lord's reversing Satan's intent to curse Israel, but they were also unaware of the snare Balaam had taught Balak to set for the young soldiers of Israel. Numbers 25 gives us the effect of Israel's sin and Revelation 2:14 gives us the hidden cause of the snare of Satan.

> *Now Israel remained in Acacia Grove, and the people began to commit harlotry with the women of Moab. They invited the people to the sacrifices of their gods, and the people ate and bowed down to their gods. So Israel was joined to Baal of Peor, and the anger of the Lord was aroused against Israel... And those who died in the plague were twenty-four thousand.... Then the Lord spoke to Moses, saying: "Harass the Midianites, and attack them; for they harassed you with their schemes by which they seduced you in the matter of Peor and in the matter of Cozbi, the daughter of a leader of Midian, their sister, who was killed in the day of the plague because of Peor."* (Numbers 25:1–3, 9, 16–18)

> *But I have a few things against you, because you have there [in your local church] those who hold the doctrine of Balaam, who taught Balak to put a stumbling block before the children of Israel, to eat things sacrificed to idols, and to commit sexual immorality.* (Revelation 2:14)

Balaam could not curse Israel and get to them from the outside. So, he taught Balak how to seduce and ensnare Israel through their own sin. Balak sent beautiful young women to invite Israel to their worship party of Baal with the promise of sex, wine, and sensual music. In the midst of this pagan ritual, Israel's young men also participated in a sacrifice to Baal. The Lord later killed all Israelites who participated in this great sin (1 Corinthians 10:8).

God takes three entire chapters (ninety-six verses) from Numbers 22–24 to give us the background scenes to this spiritual battle. This takes place just after God took three verses to recount Israel's great victory over Og, the king of Bashan in Numbers 21:33–35.

Israel was well aware of the battle they fought with Og, the King of Bashan. It required hand-to-hand combat with the enemy. However, when it came to the battle with Balaam, a spiritual battle was raging against them, and they knew nothing of it. Fellow believer, remember: Satan has secret schemes against us that we are also unaware of.

Satan has secret schemes against us that we are also unaware of.

Satan lays snares for us as well. And yet most of us are not aware of it.

We look at the struggles of our day, and we pray for God's help. We face circumstances that have turned a normal week into a trial. We take time off work for a child who is sick. The car breaks down, and we adjust our schedule to get it repaired. We are busy at church, and someone asks us to fill in for a volunteer who had to go out of town. We are so busy that we lose the margin in our lives. We feel the stress building in our emotions.

Soldiers must be aware that the battle is not just trusting God with the pressures of life, the iniquity of this world, and our own flesh. We also battle with spiritual forces in high places.

The Scripture is clear that Satan has developed strategies and schemes against us. He moves people into our lives to seduce us much like Balaam taught Balak to do to Israel's young soldiers.

Israel did not know Balaam or see Balaam or know that he was giving secret weapons to Balak to destroy theml. Because God prevented him from cursing Israel, he changed his tactics for the wages of unrighteousness. He taught Balak how to seduce Israel's soldiers with women.

Satan knows that he cannot curse you because Jesus took the curse of sin upon Himself at the Cross. You have been blessed in Christ, and there is *now no condemnation to those who are in Christ* (Romans 8:1). However, Satan knows that if he can get us to sin, then we cannot be filled with the Holy Spirit and successfully battle our flesh. Not only do we have spiritual attacks against us but also against our family and church.

Snares Satan Has Used in the Past

Snare One: At work a close friendship is established with a coworker of the opposite sex. Soon thoughts enter the mind: *You are not happy in your marriage. Your mate does not love and appreciate you. You deserve to be happy. And what is so wrong with having a friend like this at work that really understands you?* Satan has planted seeds of seduction that lead to an affair.

Snare Two: A Christian couple does their best to give their children the Christian environment for their children to grow in Christ and be protected from greater temptations of the world. Behind the scenes, Satan has a strategy against the family. Their daughter meets a classmate she is attracted to. He is not a Christian. He doesn't share the same moral values or worldview of the family. However, there is an attraction taking place, and these important differences are overlooked. Soon the young Christian is being introduced to a different world, one that is filled with sex, drinking, and drugs. A rebellious spirit is developed against her parents. Satan's strategy is successful again.

Snare Three: A pastor is leading his growing church and people are coming to Christ. There are many battles that he fights that he can see. However, behind the scenes, there are lurking battles that he cannot see. A particular woman makes an appointment to talk to the pastor about some problems she is having. She tells the pastor about her difficulties with her husband. She also shares that her husband does not physically satisfy her and she is frustrated by her lack of sexual fulfillment. At that point, the snare is set. He was already weakened spiritually by watching some pornographic material. Satan was able to use this woman to fan the fire of temptation through sexual fantasies. He is seduced, not only by this woman but also by strong demonic spiritual attacks that push him into an affair.

Arming Ourselves for Battle

What are some practical things you can do to stay strong and be prepared? How do we arm ourselves for this battle?

- **Stay in the Word.** The first line of defense in spiritual battle is always the **truth**. Paul calls the Word of God *the sword of the Spirit.* Spend time devotionally with the Lord, reading His Word to see what He has for you each day. But beyond that, study the Bible on a progressively deeper level.

  Learn the great doctrines of the Bible. I applaud you for tackling the subject of spiritual warfare by reading this book. The deeper your knowledge of spiritual truth, the more the Spirit of God can use it to strengthen your walk with Him. The Christian life is the life of Christ reproduced in the believer by the Holy Spirit according to the Word of God.

> *The first line of defense is always the **truth**. Stay in the Word.*

- **Love your spouse and children.** The home is one of Satan's premier battlefields. His attacks on marriages and parenting have been going on for centuries. But today, those battles have escalated.

  If you are married, make your marriage a top priority. Invest in spending time with each other. Go on date nights. Have deep and meaningful conversations. Resolve conflicts early. Don't let misunderstandings linger. Don't go to bed with unresolved conflict with your spouse. And above all, pray for your spouse and love him or her unconditionally. Satan loves to plant little seeds of misunderstanding that can grow into bushes of hatred.

> *Satan loves to plant little seeds of misunderstanding*
> *that can grow into bushes of hatred.*

  If you are a parent, display God's love and acceptance to your children. Teach them Bible truths but do so in a way that is engaging and reflective. In other words, don't beat them over the head with the Bible—that doesn't do anyone any good. Listen to your children. Teach them life skills that will help them succeed in life. Teach them to be on mission for the Gospel of Christ, and model that in your marriage.

- **Guard your eyes from pornography.** Because of the internet, everyone has unlimited, private access to a world of pornographic material. And it's so private that no one else knows what you are doing. But God knows ... and be sure, your sins won't remain private for long.

130

This problem is rampant. The *Promise Keepers* organization conducted a survey that revealed that 50 percent of the men who attended their rallies engaged themselves with porn within one week of attending the event. That was two decades ago. The fact that a considerable percentage of religious people have been affected by pornography causes many astute individuals to sit up and take notice.

Other statistics from several studies and articles conducted by researchers found that:

- 50% of religious men and men and 20% of religious women stated that they were addicted to pornography.
- 54% of men polled that they visited porn websites at least frequently.
- Men are more than 543% more likely to look at porn than women.
- People who have committed adultery are more likely to view pornography.
- People who have paid for sex are 270% more likely to view adult sexual content.
- Regular Church attendees are 26% less likely to look at pornography; however, 91% of people who identify themselves a "fundamentalists" are 91% more likely to look at porn. [20]

Addiction to pornography has been described as the battle of the twenty-first century. If you are involved in it, don't hide it. Get help. If you're at the early stages of involvement, stop. Talk to your pastor or a counselor. If you are a pastor, talk to someone who can help you navigate this dangerous area of temptation.

☐ **Watch out for pride.** Few things destroy you faster than success, especially spiritual success, because it makes you forget how desperately you need grace.

Do you remember the arcade game, Whack a Mole? Moles pop up all over the board, and you must take the hammer and whack them back down. The only problem is, they keep popping back up. Pride is just like that. It rears its ugly head in each of our lives time and time again. And we have to keep whacking it back down.

John Newton said, "Growth in grace primarily means growth in the realization of your need for grace and in your dependence on it." You show me a Christian whose dependence on grace is not greater than when he started, and I'll show you a Christian whose growth is artificial and fragile.

You show me a Christian whose dependence on grace is not greater than when he started, and I'll show you a Christian whose growth is artificial and fragile.

---

[20] https://www.huffingtonpost.com/elwood-d-watson/pornography-addiction-amo_b_5963460.html, October 14, 2014.

☐ **Live wisely in the world.** The book of Proverbs gives us great advice for navigating a godly life in an ungodly world. We are called to walk wisely (Ephesians 5:15), guarding our hearts in all that we do (Proverbs 4:23). Avoid unequally yoked relationships, whether they be romantic or otherwise.

Let me give you a word of balance here. We are told not to live *like the world,* but we do live *in the world.* And we're here to make a difference. Letting your light shine before men (Matthew 5:16) means bringing that light into the world's dark places. Living missionally means getting involved … just not compromising. That takes practice and discernment.

☐ **Do battle biblically.** When Jesus promised that *the gates of hell will not prevail against you* (Matthew 16:17–19), He presumed you were going into battle against the enemy. He presumed Christians would take the initiative to tear down the gates of hell. No army takes the gates off their city wall and carries them into battle. They are there for defensive purposes, which means we must take the offense against them.

☐ **Avoid places that entice the flesh.** If you are an alcoholic, don't go to a bar. If you are dating someone and sexual temptation escalates when you two are alone at night, phone a friend to come over. Avoid tempting situations. If you struggle with pornography, get a web filter for your computer. One of the best is Covenant Eyes.[21]

☐ **Be ready for battle.** Paul's advice was simple. Put on the whole armor of God and stand against the schemes of Satan (Ephesians 6:10–20). Paul pictures a first-century warrior, arming himself for battle. And he gives specific instructions about each of the seven pieces of spiritual armor that he describes:

   o The Belt of Truth. The truth He refers to is the Word of God. Mark it well: you will never survive the spiritual battle without a growing knowledge, interaction, and application of the Word of God into your life on a daily basis.

You will never survive the spiritual battle without a growing knowledge, interaction, and application of the Word of God into your life on a daily basis.

---

   o The Breastplate of Righteousness. A soldier's breastplate guarded his heart and other internal organs. It kept him safe from the attacks of the enemy. If we are trusting in our own righteousness, we will find that it's like our breastplate is made of aluminum foil—looks good, but not very protective. That's where we need the righteousness of Christ. His righteousness, not ours.

---

[21] www.covenanteyes.com.

o Shoes prepared to give the Gospel of Peace. Shoes carry the soldier into battle. *But peace? Not just any kind of peace. It's the message that men and women* can be reconciled to God through faith in Christ—that they can experience *peace with God* (Romans 5:1).

o Shield of Faith. Our shield of faith stops the *flaming darts of the evil one.* Yes, you're under attack. You may not realize it, but darts are coming at you. How do you defend yourself? *By faith!* Faith in God's power to save you, faith in God's power to protect you, and faith in God's power to use you to make a Gospel-difference in this world.

o Helmet of Salvation. A helmet goes on your head. But our head is one of our most vulnerable body parts.

Football players are realizing the effects of CTE (chronic traumatic encephalopathy) which is caused by repeated blows to the head and years of concussions. What happens when we are concussed? Our brains are damaged, and we don't think clearly. What happens when our heads are under attack spiritually? We forget the truth. And we lose the battle.

We must continually go back to the truths of our salvation. We have been bought with a price. We belong to Jesus. He has saved us. We are His sons and daughters. That's what the Gospel tells us. Remember this: we never graduate from the Gospel. It's a *lifetime curriculum.* It's not the starting point. It *is the point.* The Gospel isn't something we start with and then move on to *deeper truths.* It is the **deeper truth.**

---

*We never graduate from the Gospel. It's a **lifetime curriculum.** It's not the starting point."It **is the point.** The Gospel isn't something we start with and then move on to deeper truths. It is the **deeper truth.***

---

o Sword of the Spirit. So far, every piece of armor has been defensive. The last two are our offensive weapons. Paul defines this one for us: *the sword of the Spirit which is the Word of God.* How well do you know the Bible? So many Christians today have only a surface level understanding of the Bible.

Find a church that teaches the Bible—the truth, the whole truth, and nothing but the truth. Get in a Bible study class or a small group where you can grow in your understanding of God and His Word.

o Prayer. I believe prayer is the most neglected area for many today.

E. M. Bounds, in his classic book, *Power through Prayer,* said, "What the Church needs today is not more machinery or better, not new organizations or more and novel methods, but men whom the Holy Ghost can use — men of prayer, men mighty in prayer. The Holy Ghost does not flow through methods, but through men. He does not come on machinery, but on men. He does not anoint plans, but men—men of prayer."

As we conclude this chapter, take a moment to reflect on how you are doing in each of those areas of application:

How am I doing? Where do I need to improve? What actions should I take?
Stay in the Word.
Love your spouse and children.
Guard your eyes from pornography.
Watch out for pride.
Live wisely in the world. Do battle biblically.
Avoid places that entice the flesh.
Be ready for battle.

12   The Battle with the Midianites

From One Battle to Another

Does it ever seem that you go from fighting one battle to being immersed in another? Yeah, me too. Sometimes things just don't go the way you would like.

Add the Israelites to that list. The unseen battle with Balaam led to open war with the Midianites. It ultimately pictures the reward each soldier has coming from the Lord.

> *So Moses spoke to the people, saying, "Arm some of yourselves for war, and let them go against the Midianites to take vengeance for the LORD on Midian. A thousand from each tribe of all the tribes of Israel you shall send to the war." (Numbers 31:3–4)*

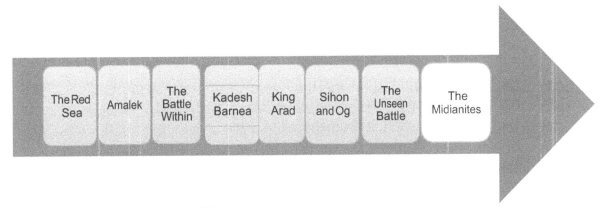

Secret Weapons and Secret Sins

The enemy is smart. He knows our weaknesses. Attempts at seduction have always been part of warfare. Just like the beautiful Delilah was able to extract the secrets of Samson's strength and military victory over the Philistines, that strategy is still being used today.

A recent exposé detailed efforts by China to gain top secret information from British intelligence officials.

> *Our source claimed the women offer the spies "great sex" and get secrets through "pillow talk." China is allegedly using 'honeytraps' to get top secret info from British intelligence officials. They are reportedly deploying "hundreds of beautiful women" who lure ex-MI6 officers into bed. Intelligence chiefs have told Prime Minister David Cameron that spies from the Far East powerhouse pose a bigger threat to national security than the Islamic State.* [22]

---

[22] *"China 'using sexy honeytrap' women to seduce former MI6 spies into giving up British secrets,"* from Mirror, November 1, 2015, written by Paul Harper.

Balaam, Babes, Booze, and Baal

God knew what Israel did not know—that His people were under attack. Moab and the Midianites attacked Israel, not with swords but with secret seductions.

The first manifestation of this attack came when God's anger was stirred against Israel and He went to war against His own people. Balaam could not get God to curse Israel, but in a counter-measure, he seemed to succeed. God's righteous anger killed twenty-four thousand soldiers of Israel. God considered Balaam's attempts to seduce Israel an act of war. He then declared war on Balaam, Moab, and the Midianites (Numbers 31: 3–4, 16).

> *Now Israel remained in Acacia Grove, and the people began to commit harlotry with the women of Moab. They invited the people to the sacrifices of their gods, and the people ate and bowed down to their gods. So Israel was joined to Baal of Peor, and the anger of the LORD was aroused against Israel.* (Numbers 25:1–3)

As Israel approached the border of the Promised Land, they were again defeated. This defeat was not because of unbelief and fear of giants as at Kadesh, but because their young soldiers did not control their lust for women.

The enemy did not tempt with whispers that they were not able to take the fortified cities of the land. Rather, he tempted them to believe they were entitled to enjoy the pleasures of the flesh that had so long been withheld from them.

At Kadesh, God let a plague kill the ten spies immediately. But that generation of soldiers who refused to take the Promised Land were all sentenced to die in the wilderness. With the pronouncement of the death sentence (the justice of God in action), God also promised that their children would inherit the Promised Land (the grace of God in action).

Now God purged the army of twenty-four thousand soldiers who had sinned in the matter of Baal Peor. In doing so, God sent a clear message that sin defeats the soldiers of God.

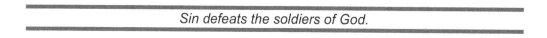

Sin defeats the soldiers of God.

Defeated by Sin: When God Fights against His People

We have already discussed the third battle in which the Lord fought against Israel over their sin with the golden calf. Now this new generation of soldiers will be reminded of God's holiness and His battle with sin in the camp of Israel. Joshua will need to remember this lesson in the future. After his first victory at Jericho, Israel will face Ai and be defeated by their small army. Why? Because of the hidden sin of one of his soldiers—Achan.

Consider some key points regarding Israel's defeat through Balaam's counsel:

☐ Balaam could not curse Israel, so he counseled Balak to seduce Israel (Numbers 31:16). This same pattern happened to the church at Pergamum in Revelation 2. Jesus tells this church, *"But I have a few things against you, because you have there [in your local church] those who hold the doctrine of Balaam, who taught Balak to put a stumbling block before the children of Israel, to eat things sacrificed to idols, and to commit sexual immorality"* (Revelation 2:14).

Among the things against this church was the fact that they fell into the same traps of idolatry and immorality. Leaders, please take note: If it could happen to a church in the first century, it can happen to a church in the twenty-first century.

☐ Moab tempted many in Israel to come to their festival to Baal where they were seduced by wine, women, and song, which led to fornication and participation in sacrifices to Baal. They slipped down the *slippery slope* and left a legacy of compromise and immorality.

They slipped down the slippery slope and left a legacy of compromise and immorality.

☐ Bowing down to Baal angered the Lord. Israel knew better. They had seen God do the miraculous in their midst. And even though this was a *new generation,* they had heard the story of the deliverance of Israel from Egypt and God's triumph at the Red Sea. Their parents received the Ten Commandments. There was no excuse for their idolatry.

And yet we, who have a much greater revelation from God, also fall into idolatry. We are the people who believe in the empty tomb and the resurrection of Jesus. We have the full revelation of the resurrected Jesus. And yet we also so quickly slip down that slippery slope and seek after other gods.

We have the full revelation of the resurrected Jesus. And yet we also so quickly slip down that slippery slope and seek after other gods.

☐ The Lord made their sin known to Moses and commanded that all the guilty leaders be publicly judged and executed to turn away the anger of the Lord from Israel. Swift judgment. Under Moses' leadership, they didn't tolerate sin in their camp any longer. The appointed judges were commanded to kill all others who were guilty. The Lord also sent a plague upon the guilty while this judgment was taking place.

While Israel was repenting with great weeping, one of the transgressors openly defied God, Moses, and Israel, by bringing a Midianite woman into his tent to commit fornication. Phinehas, the son of the high priest Eleazar, boldly took a javelin and killed them both publicly, and God stopped the plague. He also made a promise to give Phinehas and his descendants a continual priesthood.

☐ The result of that judgment was that a total of twenty-four thousand died from the executions and the plague. God called these actions by Balaam, Moab, and Midian an act of war and commanded Moses to attack them, *for they harassed you with their schemes by which they seduced you* (Numbers 25:18).

God Sent a Small Army to Defeat a Massive Army

This was Moses' last battle before God ushered him to heaven. Before he died, God commanded Moses to take vengeance on the Midianites for their seduction of Israel. There will be more principles for Joshua to learn in preparation for the conquest of Canaan.

And the LORD spoke to Moses, saying: "Take vengeance on the Midianites for the children of Israel. Afterward you shall be gathered to your people." So Moses spoke to the people, saying, "Arm some of yourselves for war, and let them go against the Midianites to take vengeance for the LORD on Midian. A thousand from each tribe of all the tribes of Israel you shall send to the war." (Numbers 31:1–4)

Joshua must learn to depend on God for directions. In the first battle at the Red Sea, God said not to fight, but in each battle that followed, Israel was to arm themselves for the battle. In most battles, all the soldiers of Israel were involved, but in this battle God would limit the number of soldiers to a small army of twelve thousand. A thousand from each tribe represented the twelve tribes of Israel against a massive army of Moab and Midian. Numbers 31 details the battle that took place.

Why would God send such a small army against an overwhelming army? What are some principles we learn from this battle in Numbers 31 against the Midianites?

☐ First, we learn that the battle belongs to the Lord. We are not to trust in our numbers and strength of our army. God plus any one individual equals a majority in any situation.

God plus any one individual equals a majority in any situation.

☐ God often allows us to be outnumbered so that we depend on Him. In doing so, the Lord receives the glory and not man. This same principle seems to be in effect when God reduced Gideon's army from thirty-two thousand to three hundred.

☐ Sometimes God sends a small force against a greater force. Sometimes God sends a great force against a small force. Don't put God into a box, saying, "This is the way You must do it," or "You didn't do it this way before!"

☐ Sometimes God sends a different man to lead His army so that we look to God and not man. God did not send Joshua to lead in this battle. He sent Phinehas, whose zeal for God stopped the plague.

☐ Sometimes holy articles were carried into battle as symbols of faith, but they were not to become objects of faith. Later when Israel carried the Ark of the Covenant into battle, they were defeated and the Ark was taken by the Philistines because the soldiers of Israel said, "The Ark will save us" (see 1 Samuel 4:3).

☐ A fearless act of faith today, though very small, may lead to greater leadership tomorrow. Phinehas, in his zeal for God's holiness, executed two in the camp of Israel and later led Israel in the destruction of thousands of the enemy.

☐ God specifically tells us that Balaam died by the sword (Numbers 31:8). God's judgment is always certain.

God's judgment is always certain.

God Supernaturally Preserved the Soldiers

Ken and Betty had become good friends in church. Connie and I went to dinner together with them many times. Ken had heart problems, and on several occasions, I rushed to the emergency room to be with him and Betty when his lungs began to fill with fluid.

On one occasion, I was reading Psalm 91 to him. He stopped me in the middle of my reading and said, "I have lived that verse, 'A thousand may fall at your side, and ten thousand at your right hand; but it shall not come near you.'" I asked Ken to tell me more. I knew he had faithfully served our country in World War II.

Ken recounted that difficult but victorious day that turned the tide of war in favor of the Allied forces against Germany. He was among the American soldiers that stormed the beaches of Normandy. He said fallen soldiers were all around him. To his left and to his right, with bullets blazing by, his comrades were falling in death. Yet, somehow God spared his life as he advanced. When the bodies were counted, 4,413 Allied troops died on the D-Day invasion. Ken said he knew the only reason he survived was that God had a plan for his life.

*And they said to Moses, "Your servants have taken a count of the men of war who are under our command, and **not a man of us is missing.**"* (Numbers 31:49, emphasis mine)

When an army goes to war against a much larger army, it is assumed that many lives will be lost. In contrast, when not one single soldier dies, it has to be assumed that it was through God's supernatural preservation. Amazingly, when Israel's army returned with the spoils of war, not one soldier was missing. They all fought with the sword and killed hundreds of thousands of the enemy, yet not one soldier of Israel died.

One commentator rightly recognized that this was a special preservation of Israel in war:

> The commanders of the troops were so grateful for this miraculous deliverance that they brought a freewill offering of gold ornaments to the LORD. They did this to make atonement, which likely means they recognized that the lack of casualties was an act of divine grace beyond anything they deserved. The total weight of their offering was 16,750 shekels (ca. 420 pounds [6,720 ounces], worth several million dollars in current United States economy). All this was brought … into the tabernacle as a memorial for the Israelites before the LORD (vv. 51–54). That is, it was a tribute to His faithfulness and blessing. [23]

> *"All this was brought … into the tabernacle as a memorial for the Israelites before the LORD. That is, it was a tribute to His faithfulness and blessing."*

The soldier must have the confidence that it is God who preserves life. When you are walking with Him, your days are numbered by Him, and only God controls when your life ends.

The Reason for the Soldier's Reward

God rewarded the soldiers with great spoils because they went to war at God's command. In other words, they were *obedient.* They didn't hesitate. Delayed obedience is simply another word for disobedience.

It is important to realize that obedience is not a work. It is really an act of faith. Because we trust God to be faithful to what He calls us to do, we obey. Our obedience is always rewarded by God because He is a rewarder of those who trust Him and diligently seek Him (Hebrews 11:6).

> *Our obedience is always rewarded by God because He is a rewarder of those who trust Him and diligently seek Him (Hebrews 11:6).*

In this battle, God made the spoils of war part of the reward for the soldiers' service to God. Notice the how great their reward was.

---

[23] Merrill, E. H. (1985). Numbers. In J. F. Walvoord & R. B. Zuck (Eds.), *The Bible Knowledge Commentary: An Exposition of the Scriptures* (Vol. 1, pp. 251-252). Wheaton, IL: Victor Books.

The booty remaining from the plunder, which the men of war had taken, was six hundred and seventy-five thousand sheep, seventy-two thousand cattle, sixty-one thousand donkeys, and thirty-two thousand persons in all, of women who had not known a man intimately. (Numbers 31:32–35)

1. *Motives Matter*

Motive is always important to God. Balaam *seemed* godly when he told Balak that he was not a prophet for hire, and even if he was given a fortune, he could not speak but that which God spoke to him. As we have already pointed out, the New Testament reveals his real motive in going with Balak was *"the wages of unrighteousness."*

Motive is always important to God.

In contrast, the motive of Phinehas and the small army of twelve thousand was their zeal and obedience to God. This motive was rewarded by God. God searches the heart. When we go to battle against principalities, powers, and spiritual wickedness in high places, we must have a pure motive before God.

We do not serve God for reward ... but God rewards those who serve Him. It is the character of God to reward those who diligently seek Him (Heb. 11:6). The principle is that the *"The laborer is worthy of his wages."* If God extended this principle to the ox, how much more so to the servants of God.

> *For the Scripture says, "You shall not muzzle an ox while it treads out the grain," and, "The laborer is worthy of his wages."* (1 Timothy 5:18)

God did not send Israel to war at their own expense, and God did not withhold the reward of their sacrifice from them. God is not like Pharaoh, who made Israel slaves and required service without reward. In fact, when God delivered Israel from Egypt, He ensured that they received their back wages plus interest for their years of slavery as they came out with great treasures and spoils of Egypt (see Exodus 12:35–36).

> *Whoever goes to war at his own expense? Who plants a vineyard and does not eat of its fruit? Or who tends a flock and does not drink of the milk of the flock?* (1 Corinthians 9:7)

Jesus taught that if we do our deeds to be seen by men, then we have no reward in heaven (Matthew 6:1–4). Motive matters to God.

2. Faithful Service Matters

Faithful service matters to God as well. The fact that God will reward His servants is a constant theme in the New Testament.

While serving God on earth, we may face many trials and persecution and seem forgotten by man. However, Jesus taught that we should rejoice at such persecution knowing that our reward in heaven will be great (Matthew 5:10–12). The servants of Christ are told that Jesus is coming again, and He will reward each believer *according to his works* (Matthew 16:27).

Joshua and Israel will have to first fight for God's glory with the assurance that God rewards His servants. Each battle is different, and God designates the spoils of war (Numbers 31:25–52). Sometimes God says that the spoils were to be destroyed; sometimes they were dedicated to God only; sometimes they were to be distributed among the army first with the largest share going to those who fought; sometimes they were shared with all. Joshua will later learn at Jericho that even one soldier taking the spoils of war that God did not designate to Israel would lead to defeat.

Here is a great principle to remember as we follow Jesus: Serve and obey God with joy and faithfulness because you love Him. Trust God with His rewards, whether now on earth or in the future in heaven. God sees the heart.

> *Serve and obey God with joy and faithfulness because you love Him. Trust God with His rewards, whether now on earth or in the future in heaven. God sees the heart.*

3. Obey Even When You Don't Understand

The soldier must trust God with His orders even when he does not understand why.

> *But Moses was angry with the officers of the army, with the captains over thousands and captains over hundreds, who had come from the battle. And Moses said to them: "Have you kept all the women alive? Look, these women caused the children of Israel, through the counsel of Balaam, to trespass against the LORD in the incident of Peor, and there was a plague among the congregation of the LORD. Now therefore, kill every male among the little ones, and kill every woman who has known a man intimately.* (Numbers 31:14–17.

Moses reflected God's heart and judgment in this battle with the Midianites. If God hates sin, then his servants should hate sin also. Moses understood that these women were the cause of Israel's trespass. God pronounced judgment and plague upon the men of Israel who committed sexual immorality. Now that same judgment was upon the women who seduced them.

It seems strange that Phinehas, who had the same zeal as Moses the previous day in the camp when he executed God's judgment, may have amended God's judgment on the battlefield by not executing the guilty women. Remember, it was God who selected Phinehas to lead this battle instead of Joshua or Caleb. What happened on the battlefield that may have changed Phinehas' zeal? Did he allow the voices of the soldiers under his command to temper his judgment? (Remember King Saul allowed his soldiers to amend the orders of God to utterly destroy the Amalekites. See 1 Samuel 15.)

The individual zealous act of Phinehas in the camp is not as hard as the continual zeal for the Lord on the battlefield, where many voices seek to influence your leadership. Most pastors will tell you that it is easier to be zealous for the Lord behind the pulpit, but it is far more difficult in the committee meeting with many voices of influence.

It is easy for us to rationalize God's commands when there is the influence of many. The soldier must be the same in the camp as he is in the battlefield. There will be times in our Christian lives that our emotions are stressed, our bodies are fatigued, and our wills are weakened by the long fight. Then a circumstance arises in which we do not understand why. When you face such a time, it may be best just to keep marching and obeying the last orders you received from your commander in chief. Someone said it well, "Do not question in the night the clear directions you received in the light."

Alfred Lord Tennyson's famous poem, "The Charge of the Light Brigade," recounts the story of soldiers obeying orders in the face of imminent death in the Crimean War of 1854. The most famous stanza of that poem says,

> *"Theirs not to make reply,*
> *Theirs not to reason why,*
> *Theirs but to do and die."*

Moses had clear orders from God regarding the judgment upon these women and God's vengeance against the Midianites. Phinehas' leadership was not to reason why, but to lead his army in carrying out the orders he had received from Moses. Leadership is not easy, and it is not for those who do not understand the soldier's chain of command. [24]

Principle: The soldier must understand God's chain of command. He or she must submit to those over them in the Lord. The Word of God is his final authority and marching

---

[24] We are not told anything about the decision on the battlefield as to why the women were brought back alive. It seems that Phinehas was given the leadership in this battle (Num. 31:6). We are told that Moses was angry with the appointed officers and captains (Num. 31:14).

orders. He will at times hear many voices that challenge his leadership. He will at times not know the answers to every difficult circumstance he faces.

The soldier must understand God's chain of command.
He or she must submit to those over them in the Lord.

---

4. The Soldier Is Always under Authority

The soldier's reason must never supersede God's wisdom. Moses was the meekest man on earth. His patience and love for his people was unparalleled. He interceded for Israel many times when God would have destroyed them. He was even willing to be blotted out of God's book to spare Israel.

> *Oh, these people have committed a great sin, and have made for themselves a god of gold! Yet now, if You will forgive their sin—but if not, I pray, blot me out of Your book which You have written.* (Exodus 32:31–32)

In no way do we see this compassionate servant shepherd as a Hitler-type despot, a mass murderer who delighted in the pain or torment of people. Yet we see Moses without hesitation ordering the death of all the Midianites except the young virgins.

> *Now therefore, kill every male among the little ones, and kill every woman who has known a man intimately. But keep alive for yourselves all the young girls who have not known a man intimately.* (Numbers 31:17–18)

How do we reconcile our God of love and mercy with these passages where God ordered the complete destruction of the nations of the Promised Land? The critics of the Bible have used God's order of complete destruction of the nations of Canaan as proof that the Bible is a myth and our God is a cruel monster. (We will look closer at the subject of God ordering the destruction of nations of the Promised Land in Book Two.) Consider the example of Jesus when the Pharisees expected Him to stone the woman taken in adultery –He forgave her. Remember, the weapons of our warfare are not physical but spiritual.)

The example of Moses was extremely important for Joshua's training in the conquest of the Promised Land. He must not repeat what had just happened on the battlefield with the sparing of the women of Midianites who were marked for judgment.

Where was Joshua's allegiance? Was it with Phinehas on the battlefield, or was he with Moses? If Phinehas led Israel into this battle, how did Joshua handle what seemed like a demotion? Was Joshua the leader of the thousand selected from his tribe Ephraim? Was he, like his mentor Moses, without envy or jealousy, and desiring others to grow and experience leadership?

Joshua learned from Israel's incomplete obedience. When he later led Israel against Jericho, all that breathed were destroyed except Rahab and her family because of her conversion (Joshua 6:21).

God marked the nations of the Promised Land for judgment after waiting over four hundred years until *their iniquity was full.* God commanded Joshua in Deuteronomy 20:16–18 to carry out His judgment on these nations. Like Moses, he obeyed. He learned from the failure in the battle with the Midianites and was faithful to carry out the orders of God, his commander in chief. He did not place his reason above the wisdom of God. God alone knew the future, and the greater destruction that these nations would bring to both Israel and the world. As a good soldier, he simply obeyed.

> *So Joshua conquered all the land: the mountain country and the South and the lowland and the wilderness slopes, and all their kings; he left none remaining, but utterly destroyed all that breathed, as the LORD God of Israel had commanded.* (Joshua 10:40)

As a good soldier, he simply obeyed.

---

5. *The Soldier Must Defend the Faith*

Satan continually attacks the Bible and accuses God in the minds of the lost world. This is especially true in regards to God commanding Joshua to completely destroy all the nations of the Promised Land.

The soldier must put on the whole armor of God and use the Sword of the Spirit, which is the Word of God against enemy attacks (Ephesians 6:10–18). We are told to always be ready to give an answer for the reason of the hope that is in us. (1 Peter 3:15).

Sometimes when we do not understand the *why* of what God is asking us to do. We simply need to remember *Who gave the command* and trust God.

Sometimes when we do not understand the why of what God is asking us to do. We simply need to remember Who gave the command and trust God.

 **Application**

Discuss one principle from this chapter.

13　Give Me This Mountain!

The End of the Beginning

Do you remember your graduation from high school or college? Chances are there was a lot of pomp and circumstance. Your family was so proud of you. And there was a commencement speaker who used a lot of clichés and talked about "the beginning of the rest of your life." And chances are you didn't listen very well. But if you did, you would have heard something like this:

1. Today marks a new beginning.
2. You're prepared; you're trained; you're ready.
3. Now go conquer the world!

The book of Deuteronomy acts much like a graduation speech for the nation of Israel. And Moses was the commencement speaker. Because of his previous unbelief, Moses was barred from entry into the land. However, as a good leader, he was committed to preparing this new generation to go into the land. And his message to them was similar:

1. Today marks a new beginning.
2. You're prepared; you're trained; you're ready.
3. God is with you; He is faithful; He has promised you this land; you can trust Him.
4. Now go conquer the world!

You obviously notice the one addition to the commencement message. It is the divine element: the promises of God, the presence of God, the power of God! That's what makes the difference. It always is.

The promises of God, the presence of God, the power of God!
That's what makes the difference. It always is.

When you realize that God is with you, you become invincible. You can do anything and everything He calls you to do. You find yourself agreeing with Paul, *"I can do all things through Christ who strengthens me"* (Philippians 4:13).

In Deuteronomy, Moses rehearsed the lessons Israel learned from the battles along the way. Scholars tell us that Deuteronomy contains three sermons Moses gave to Israel before he died. These were his last words after leading the nation for forty years. What did he want them to remember? What was essential as this new generation entered the Promised Land and fought the battles before them?

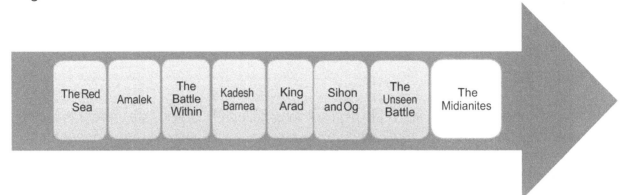

Moses wanted them to know that:

1. Truth revealed must be truth that is obeyed.

   Surely I have taught you statutes and judgments, just as the Lord my God commanded me, that you should act according to them in the land which you go to possess. Therefore be careful to observe them; for this is your wisdom and your understanding in the sight of the peoples who will hear all these statutes, and say, 'Surely this great nation is a wise and understanding people' (Deuteronomy 4:5–6).

   It's one thing to know the truth. It's quite another to obey it. God's people are distinctively marked— not so much by what they know, but by what they do.

2. Diligently walk with God and trust Him every step of the way.

   Only take heed to yourself, and diligently keep yourself, lest you forget the things your eyes have seen, and lest they depart from your heart all the days of your life. And teach them to your children and your grandchildren, especially concerning the day you stood before the Lord your God in Horeb, when the Lord said to me, "Gather the people to Me, and I will let them hear My words, that they may learn to fear Me all the days they live on the earth, and that they may teach their children." (Deuteronomy 4:9–10)

3. Seek Him always, and never let the fire burn out on your love for Jesus.

   But from there you will seek the Lord your God, and you will find Him if you seek Him with all your heart and with all your soul. (Deuteronomy 4:29)

How did the nation respond? Chapter 4, verse 47 says that *they took possession of the land.* The nation was ready. They were prepared. A mountain of a challenge lay before them, and they would learn much more. We will walk that journey with them in the second volume of this series. But as we close this volume, I ask you, "Are you ready? Are you prepared to move ahead? Will you trust God for the battles today and tomorrow?"

Are you ready? Are you prepared to move ahead?
Will you trust God for the battles today and tomorrow?

How to Claim a Mountain

Allow me to jump ahead in the story a few years. The nation finds themselves well on the way to possessing the land. But they still faced a few battles. In Joshua chapter 14, the emphasis moves from Joshua to Caleb. And the focus is on the hill country where the giants had been seen when Joshua and Caleb were spying out the land.

It was perhaps the toughest territory to conquer. And Caleb was not the same forty-year-old who had come to spy out the land in Numbers 13. He is now eighty-five years old. But Caleb was confident that with the power of God he would be able to take this tough territory. He wanted the mountain! (Joshua 14:12–15).

In the last chapter in this volume, instead of focusing on the battles Joshua and his forces were facing, I would like to focus on *you* and the battles you are facing.

If you remember back to the introduction of this book, I talked about how some of our battles are brought on by circumstances, some are brought on by sin, and some are the result of spiritual warfare. On page two of the introduction, I had you list the battles you are going through right now and which category those battles fell into. Now I would like you to go back and update that chart.

- [ ] What has changed (if anything) since you first wrote those words on the page?
- [ ] And also, what lessons have you learned over the course of this study?

The Battle	The Source	Changes in the Battle	Lessons I've Learned

As we close this study, I would like to give you three words of encouragement. Each of us has battles we are facing. Our natural temptation is to attack those battles in our own flesh. But that will never work. Jesus said, *"Apart from Me, you can do nothing"* (John 15:5). The battle is not *ours;* the battle *belongs to the Lord.* And He is the One who must fight for us and with us.

Confidence

The first word of encouragement is *confidence.* But don't be misled. It is not self-confidence. It is a God-based confidence. It is a confidence that says, "My God is with me, and my God can do anything."

Caleb understood this when he said, *"Give me that mountain"* (Joshua 14:12). He knew from forty-five years earlier that God had given them the mountain. The enemies that possessed that part of the land, though they looked fierce, were no match for Caleb and his fellow-fighters.

Some of you are advanced in years. You've made a bunch of trips around the sun. And if you are like me, you may be tempted to say, "My best years are behind me." That is **not true!** May I say it clearly: if you are still breathing, God can use you. He can use you to pray, He can use you to mentor and inspire others, and He can use you far beyond your dreams.

> *May I say it clearly: if you are still breathing, God can use you.*
> *He can use you to pray, He can use you to mentor and inspire others,*
> *and He can use you far beyond your dreams.*

Your confidence will be shaken if you look to yourself. Your confidence will *never* be shaken if you keep your eyes focused on Jesus.

Here's what Caleb said after eighty-five trips around the sun:

> *Now then, just as the Lord promised, he has kept me alive for forty-five years since the time he said this to Moses, while Israel moved about in the desert. So here I am today, eighty-five years old!* (Joshua 14:10)

Caleb's faith in God was not shaken by the circumstances he encountered. The battles he faced were merely opportunities for God to display His great power and faithfulness.

> *Caleb's faith in God was not shaken by the circumstances he encountered.*
> *The battles he faced were merely opportunities*
> *for God to display His great power and faithfulness.*

150

What about you? Are you prone to give into fear like the other ten spies did? They lacked faith —and because of their unbelief, they never entered the Promised Land. If you are not strong in faith, you will never see God win the battles in your life. Build up your faith. Get to know God better each day. Read His Word. Learn His ways. Ask Him for the faith to face the mountains in your life.

Take a moment right now and pray. Pray that God's Spirit might speak and show you the next steps He wants you to take. What is God saying to your heart?

Strength

In the same way that confidence is never self-confidence (it is always **God-confidence**), strength is never self-strength, it is always **strength in the Lord.**

Caleb said, *"I am still as strong today as the day Moses sent me out"* (Joshua 14:11). Had Caleb been overdosing on energy drinks? Did he raid the GNC store at Jericho? No, he knew where his strength came from. It came from God.

Some of the strongest people I know are those whose outlook on life is shaped by the Word of God. Relying on His promises—that cannot fail—gives strength and purpose to every believer. Paul put it this way: *And do not be drunk with wine, in which is dissipation; but be filled with the Spirit* (Ephesians 5:18). When we are filled and empowered by God's Spirit, He gives us inner strength. This is exactly what Paul prayed for earlier in this same book:

> *For this reason I bow my knees to the Father of our Lord Jesus Christ, from whom the whole family in heaven and earth is named, that He would grant you, according to the riches of His glory,* **to be strengthened with might through His Spirit in the inner man,** *that Christ may dwell in your hearts through faith; that you, being rooted and grounded in love, may be able to comprehend with all the saints what is the width and length and depth and height—to know the love of Christ which passes knowledge; that you may be filled with all the fullness of God.* (Ephesians 3:14–19)

Strength. Inner strength. That's right where I need it. And so do you.

When we are filled and empowered by God's Spirit, He gives us inner strength. Strength. Inner strength. That's right where I need it. And so do you.

Take a moment and go back over this prayer. Pray it back to God. Personalize it. Pray it for yourself and for those closest to you. Pray it for your pastor and church leaders.

Faithfulness

Caleb saw what God did in parting the Red Sea. He was a witness to the miraculous fall of the walls of Jericho. He knew what God had done. And because He knew what God had faithfully done in the past, it gave him great confidence for what God would do in the future.

Caleb was willing to tackle the tough territory. He knew what God had promised forty years earlier. And he knew that God's promise hadn't changed. *Faithful is He who calls you, who will also bring it to pass* (1 Thessalonians 5:24). And as a result, Caleb had enough for himself and his descendants. The benefits of his mountain climbing poured over into the lives of those around him.

The benefits of his mountain climbing poured over into the lives of those around him.

What has God promised to you? What has He called you to do? I know of a man in his sixties who had felt called into the ministry when he was young. But he always resisted the call. Finally, when it came time to retire, he simply couldn't shake the conviction he had felt years earlier. He went to his pastor and told him what was going in. With wisdom, the pastor said, "So, what's stopping you from doing that now?" The man eventually went to seminary and became an associate pastor at his church. What did he learn from that whole experience? He said, "God is faithful. His calling never changed, despite my years of disobedience. I'm grateful that He never gave up on me."

Our Father wants us to be God-confident, trusting in His strength rather than our own, and relying on His faithfulness rather than our self-effort. As we close, take the following three questions before the Lord and write down what He is teaching you in these areas.

In what ways have I learned to be God-confident rather than self-confident?

In what ways have I learned to trust in God's strength rather than my own?

In what ways have I learned to rely on God's faithfulness rather than my self-effort?

Feel free to contact us at the address and phone number below for more information or to place your order today.

Truman Herring
Phone: 561-350-4451
www.trumanherringministries.com

Other Books by Truman Herring

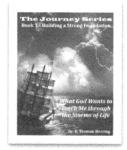

Journey Series – Book 1 – Building a Strong Foundation – The moment we received the Lord Jesus, we began an amazing journey of grade with God. This journey is with purpose ad design to lead us into maturity and fruitfulness. Often overlooked is how God uses the storms of life in the process of growth. This study is design to help us understand six key principles of growing in the storms of life in our journey of walking with Jesus. ***Cost: $19.99 each plus shipping***

Journey Series – Book 2 – Growing Deeper – Following Jesus means that God is bringing people, places, and events into our life with purpose. This book is to help us better understand and enjoy our Journey with Christ. In this book we deal with how Jesus progressively leads his followers to deeper faith and abiding fruitfulness. In the first storm, Jesus would be present in the boat with them. In this second storm, Jesus will send them into the storm alone. ***Cost: $19.99 each plus shipping***

Sound the Alarm – Many Bible believing Christians are grieved and are deeply concerned about the future of America. This book examines the principles of God's judgment of nations and seeks to answer the question: Will God judge America? This book is also a call to hope and prayer that God will revive His Church and heal our nation before it is too late. ***Cost: $19.99 each plus shipping***

Sound the Alarm – A Call to Prayer – is a sample edition of 21 of the chapters from Sound the Alarm. To focus on Hope and Intercession for America by including a section at the end of each devotion for you to include your prayers or thoughts of what God is saying to you personally. God is calling many Christians to intercede for America and His Church. Will you be one of them? ***Cost: $10.00 each plus shipping***

Responsive Hearts – Fine Tuning our Hearts to God's Heart

Why do bad things happen to God's people? If He loves us, why do we have troubles and trials? God could easily protect us from our trials and problems. Yet, God does not. He could, but He doesn't, so there must be a reason. God is working in our lives to fine-tune our hearts to His heart. He tenderly develops responsive, sensitive hearts in His children. By faith, we see a bright future even in our dark days. Loyal, responsive hearts are the ones through whom God works. ***Cost: $15.00 each plus shipping***

God's Greater Purpose in Christ – How Do I Fit In?

Have you found yourself asking, "Do I have a purpose in life? Where do I fit in? Can my life really impact others?" God's greater purpose is "in Christ," and never apart from Jesus Christ. Any other purpose, no matter how celebrated or successful, is a cheap substitute. By studying the lives of several Bible personalities, whose unique purposes were outlined for them before they were born, we can discover that this same God has a unique purpose for us as well. This book is written to help you discover God's greater purpose for your life! ***Cost: $15.00 each plus shipping***

Hannah's Journey from Barrenness to Blessings – Strong, Fruitful, Fulfilled

What is the secret to being "fruitful?" What does that really mean in your life? Have you desired a more fruitful walk with God? ***Strong, Fruitful, Fulfilled*** magnifies God's great work in the life of Hannah, but it shares the eternal principles that God designed for both men and women. The principles of Scripture drawn from Hannah's struggles and journey of faith will answer your questions. ***Cost: $15.00 each plus shipping***

A Ministry That Pleases God – Learning to Do God's Work God's Way

What's a leader to do when it comes to ministry? There are a lot of suggestions out there for pastors and Christian leaders today. But how should a leader . . . lead? This is a book for leaders, but more specifically, it is about doing God's ministry God's way. It is written to ministry leaders – not only pastors and church planters, but also for the many other leaders in our churches today. This book reflects a growing conviction that ministry should be done according to God's way in the power of God's Spirit.

This book is currently in six languages and is given free to church planters in India, Nepal, Myanmar, and some countries in Africa. Cost: $15.00 each plus shipping

Made in USA - Kendallville, IN
75323_9780997923438
08.23.2022 1351